SERVING OUR CHILDREN

SERVING OUR
CHILDREN

Charter Schools and the Reform of
American Public Education

KEVIN P. CHAVOUS

Chair, Council of the District
of Columbia's Committee on
Education, Libraries and Recreation

CAPITAL
BOOKS, INC.
Sterling, Virginia

Capital Books, Inc.
P.O. Box 605
Herndon, Virginia 20172-0605

Front cover photo by Jim Harrison, Copyright © 1998

Author photo by Kea Prather, Copyright © 2004

ISBN 1-931868-69-7 (alk.paper)

Library of Congress Cataloging-in-Publication Data

Chavous, Kevin P.
    Serving our children : charter schools and the reform of American
    public education / Kevin P. Chavous.—1st ed.
        p.   cm.—(A Capital currents book)
    Includes bibliographical references and index.
    ISBN 1-931868-69-7 (alk. paper)
    1. Charter schools—Washington (D.C.)   2. Public schools—Washington
(D.C.)   3. Educational change—Washington (D.C.)   I. Title.   II. Series.
LB2806.36.C57   2004
371.01—dc22   2003022652

Printed in the United States of America on acid-free paper that meets the American National Standards Institute Z39-48 Standard.

First Edition

10   9   8   7   6   5   4   3   2   1

This book is dedicated to my parents,
Harold and Bettie Chavous
and to the memory of my in-laws,
Leonard and Berneice Bass.

CONTENTS

FOREWORD

America is at a crossroads in the field of education. Across
the nation, citizens bemoan the state of public education,
but wait for our leaders to solve the problem. We intuitively
know that our current approach is not working for far too
many of our children, particularly our poorest children, a
disproportionate number of whom are children of color. Yet
many are fearful of challenging the status quo. In *Serving Our
Children*, Councilmember Kevin P. Chavous addresses those
fears and explores the potential of charter schools as agents
for real change in public education.

From my vantage point, this book offers a perspective
that is long overdue. Having promoted parental choice
around the country and as superintendent of schools in Milwaukee, I view the charter school effort as both a social
movement and educational strategy. Ralph Turner said that,
"a significant social movement becomes possible when there
is a revision in the manner in which a substantial group of
people look at some misfortune, seeing it no longer as a
misfortune warranting charitable consideration, but as an injustice which is intolerable in this society." I believe that the
crux of the charter school idea is the realization that a grave
injustice has been perpetrated against our children, particularly our poorest children of color. The unwillingness or inability of so many schools and school systems to educate
them constitutes an injustice that cannot be dealt with
through charitable notions and platitudes such as "all children can learn." In fact, it must be dealt with by actions that
will lead to a totally new educational reality for all children,

but particularly for the children who have been, and continue to be, ill-served by our current systems of education. Councilmember Chavous argues that we must face the inequity of how our kids are treated in school like it is "the last civil rights challenge" in America.

Charter schools are also an educational strategy, and we have to be focused on creating excellent learning environments. I say learning environments, because I don't want to emphasize schools. What we have to do is understand that the kinds of environments that we need to create do not have to be schools in the traditional sense. In fact, the industrial age paradigm which suggests that all learning takes place at the same time in the same way needs to be exploded. Charter schools are one of the instruments to change that paradigm and create these new learning environments.

Serving Our Children gives us cogent, real life examples of successful charter schools in the District of Columbia. These examples aid us in our mission to redefine public education. Councilmember Chavous's honest, thoughtful treatment of the D.C. experience with school choice is a story all need to heed. It is especially rare that an elected official takes a stand for meaningful systemic change in traditional education. Throughout his career and in his book, Councilmember Chavous demonstrates that he has the courage to take on the historical institutional resistance that has thwarted efforts to change public education. He offers practical hands-on solutions that parents and teachers will eagerly embrace.

Howard Fuller, Ph.D.

INTRODUCTION

"So long as they disable our children in the area of education, we
can never be free."

—Thurgood Marshall

I had served on the District of Columbia City Council for
three years when Councilmember Bill Lightfoot began
speaking of change and retirement. Bill had already served
on the City Council for four years when I was sworn in on
January 2, 1993. In my early days he had been a generous
mentor; in the latter days, also a good friend. As a politician,
he had been consistent, fervent, and unwaveringly optimistic
in a city long mired in fiscal, political, and social inadequa-
cies. One morning over coffee, I asked a question I had been
meaning to ask for some time: "Do you have any regrets?"

"Education." His answer came without hesitation.

Bill's one major regret was that he had never sought the
chairmanship of the education committee. "We spend all of
our time preventing disasters in our wards—whether it's a
fiscal crisis or a crime wave. We're always putting out the fires
and thinking that issues like education are a luxury. What we
never stopped to consider was the connection between lack
of opportunities and access to education, and what was play-
ing out in the streets—that perhaps education is the root of
our problems."

It was a catalytic moment for me—one that made me re-
consider why I had entered public service in the first place:
surely not to move defensively from day to day, from one
disaster to the next. My colleagues and I had always acknowl-

1

edged that education was a "top priority," but given the almost single-minded focus we had to place on other, more pressing issues, the attention to D.C. schools amounted to not much more than lip service.

In 1996, the Education Committee was run by Hilda Mason. A former teacher and school board member, Hilda had fought the battle for education for many years and had served the city well. Then in her eighties, unfortunately she did not have the energy to take on the dramatic reforms that were needed at the time. Schools were receiving little, if any, oversight. Encouraged by my friend's words, I decided to lobby for the committee chairmanship, as did another junior councilmember, Kathy Patterson. That no senior councilmember was interested in the post was surely telling.

More than a few colleagues and supporters tried to dissuade me from seeking the position:

"It's a no-win situation," I was told.

"It will hurt you politically."

"The schools are in really bad shape, and their problems will follow your career."

"Leave education alone; you'll never win."

I was surprised by how many earnest, bright people seemed to share the view that education was a political black hole. At the same time, I began to pay more attention to the rhetoric of the presidential elections in process at the time. All the candidates claimed that education was a top priority, but a closer look at their proposals revealed no new, progressive ideas.

It was then that I started to examine the overall problems of the D.C. school system with an eye toward change. Despite all the advice to the contrary, I fought for the committee chairmanship and won. In the years since, I have worked with parents, educators, and policymakers to improve learning in the District's classrooms. I have seen trends in education come and go. I am convinced that real reform in education must be both radical and innovative. And I have supported countless innovations—some successful, many less so. Of these successful innovations, only a handful—community-hub schools, mandatory pre-primary, longer school days and year, a more rigorous curriculum at an earlier age—have the capacity to effect long-term, sustainable reform in our education system, and I believe that charter schools create an environment for those things to occur by freeing principals, teachers, and parents from shackles. School autonomy is a prerequisite to meaningful change in our schools.

It is an unfortunate reality that American children growing up in the throes of the high-tech revolution are being taught by a public school system that was put in place during the nineteenth century Industrial Revolution and has changed very little since. From the perspective of a politician, education is hard work. It requires understanding on both substantive and political levels, and an aggressive thrust for change in bureaucracies that are some of the most entrenched in government. In the District, the school bureaucracy involves roughly a billion dollars and several thousand employees—some committed to change, but others so entangled in bureaucratic malaise that they will resist change with their very last breath. Breaking up the bureaucracy, I have found, is a full-time endeavor.

Like other states, D.C.'s experiment with charter schools has had mixed results. When I took over the chairmanship of the D.C. Council's Education Committee, the District had the authorizing legislation, but no charter schools. In six short years, we have gone from zero to forty charter schools and we now have almost $140 million set aside exclusively for charters. Some of these schools, founded with ambitious, visionary mandates, burned out quickly, with disappointing results, fiscal mismanagement or other mishaps. A few, however, have not only withstood the formative years but also thrived. Each of these exemplary schools provides valuable lessons that can serve to promote fundamental change in our public school systems.

As a councilmember, education committee chairman,

and father of two sons, I have had the opportunity to observe the education system from many angles. This book represents several years of critical thinking, analysis, and synthesis. The problems in education are well known and widely acknowledged, and I will discuss them only briefly. What I hope to do with some degree of success is to provide a holistic framework of short- and long-term solutions to the shortcomings in our education system, using charter schools as a primary foundation. I will share with you anecdotes, research, interviews, and other resources I have encountered in my work. It is my hope that this book will in some way advance teaching and learning in our schools.

CHAPTER 1

The Last Civil Rights Challenge

"I knew I was truly free when I could read a book"

—Frederick Douglass

We need new and radical solutions to reform our public schools. So-called solutions are introduced with dizzying speed from all sorts of likely and unlikely quarters, including politicians from both sides of the political aisle. During each election cycle, politicians hold education aloft as their crusade du jour, promising transformation! reform! accountability! Unfortunately, once they're elected most fall short of action. Some are sidetracked by special interests, and others are sucked in by bureaucratic quicksand.

Often, the solutions have been heard before and the methods tried before. Many do not go far enough. Drastic situations call for dramatic measures. Demanding more and more money for a rotting bureaucracy will not work! Vigorously assessing children who are in no position to learn and then penalizing their schools by withholding funding will not work! Democrats are predictable in their demands for more and more money. Republicans continue to call for more assessment and testing, and their clamoring for vouchers as the end-all solution. Neither party has shown the vision for the holistic and dramatic solutions needed to rescue our drowning schools.

When done right, school enables children to grasp and

embrace the beauty of the educational experience at an early age. Encouraged and supported children foster the process because they like school and are infinitely more likely to be successful adolescents and adults. Never has it been more true that

> There are powerful ideas and promising experiments struggling to take root amid the fire-bombed landscape of our school system, but the weight of the status quo is so enormous that it often crushes them before they can make a real difference.[1]

That crushing weight, of course, is the education monopoly and special interests.

For over 150 years, traditional public education has operated in essentially the same manner. The rudiments of American public education began with the belief that as a nation we needed to inculcate certain values and mores in our children. Thomas Jefferson took this idea and expanded on it by declaring that at least one citizen in every four- to five-square-mile radius was to provide the area's children with instruction in the sciences, arts, and morals of society. America's public schools were founded on the notion that for a democracy to work, all children need to be able to read, write, and compute, and all children must understand their responsibilities and rights as citizens.

The Jeffersonian approach continued until the 1830s, when Boston became the first jurisdiction to institute compulsory education sanctioned by the state. Every child was required to attend school. And schools taught curricula consisting mainly of arts and sciences, some understanding of democratic processes and the moral way of conducting oneself. Later, John Dewey advanced the progressive educational theory of the twentieth century, suggesting that in a democracy, education must engage with and enlarge the everyday human experience.

Incredibly, for a century and a half, there has been little

substantive change in public education. In America's public classrooms, the classic approach remains essentially the same as it was years ago: one-size-fits-all with a core curriculum of subjects presented to all students in largely the same manner. Students are divided by age and taught according to this curriculum. And they are promoted based on their perceived mastery of subjects. Or worse, they are advanced as part of a tacit social promotion system that serves no one—particularly not the children themselves.

What many people do not know is that the civil rights movement got its legs in the area of education. Throughout history, withholding education has been used by oppressors to keep the oppressed down. This was most blatantly demonstrated when it was against the law to teach slaves to read. However, the slaves understood the importance of learning to read, so they risked beatings and hangings to teach each other to read by candlelight when the master was asleep. Interestingly, after the Civil War and during Reconstruction, there were concentrated efforts to ensure that while blacks were entitled to some form of education, they did not receive an equal or superior education.

From this philosophy arose the 1896 Supreme Court decision *Plessy v. Ferguson,* asserting that "separate but equal" facilities for blacks and whites were legal. Booker T. Washington and W.E.B. Dubois, two of the most prominent figures in African American history, were caught up in a continuing debate about whether blacks should accept the status quo and work to better themselves (Washington), or take a more active role in bringing about equal rights and integration (Dubois).

In the twentieth century, during the period of "separate-but-equal" education, it became clear exactly how unequal education was, particularly for people of lower economic status. When Thurgood Marshall joined the NAACP Legal Defense Fund, his work really ignited the civil rights movement of the 1960s. Marshall would file lawsuits in places like Texas, Oklahoma, and Virginia to challenge the separate-but-equal laws and argue that every American child should have equal access to a quality education. It took the 1954 Supreme Court decision *Brown v. Board of Education* to establish that separate-but-equal has no place in our society, and that all children have a right to a quality education.

The civil rights movement took that decision and applied the principle to public accommodations, the right to vote, and other benefits of citizenship. Today, while the law is clear and all Americans legally have the right to an education, there is an inherent disparity in the education offerings provided to our children. Much of that disparity is based on socioeconomic status. If your parents have means and you come from an affluent background, chances are good that you will receive a high-quality education. If you come from the lower economic segments of our society and are dependent on the public school system, there is a reasonable chance you will receive less than a solid education.[2] National studies of educational progress and assessments conducted in elementary, middle, and high schools confirm that the achievement scores of African American and Hispanic children consistently fall below those of their white peers. These minority youth tend to score significantly lower on vocabulary, reading, mathematics, and scholastic aptitude.[3]

These disparities in educational attainment present a new reality for our nation. In effect, our need to fix public education presents a new civil rights challenge for America. One of the most enduring images of the civil rights era in my memory occurred when I was ten years old. My father and I were watching the evening news, when the grainy image of an elderly black man emerged on the screen. He had been walking home from church when several white men attacked him suddenly and brutally. They beat him with bats and kicked, punched, and taunted him. The old man had tried to get up, to keep walking, following every blow that knocked him to the ground. Despite his resolve, he was beaten to a bloody, unconscious pulp. I do not remember the words of the newscaster, but I will never forget the images.

What I saw changed my world. It was 1966. The images had come from Selma, Alabama. The country was in the midst of a social upheaval. My ten-year-old mind struggled to grasp the barbarism: Why were the men beating the old man? Why wasn't he fighting back? How could the police let this happen? Why didn't someone help?

Although I was aware of the civil rights problem in America, following that newscast I felt rage for the first time in my life. I could not understand why every black person in America, including my father, wasn't in the streets fighting for freedom.

"Daddy, let's go find us some white people to beat up." My logic was fast and furious—that of a young boy. My father raised his head with a deep frown.

My father had grown up on a farm in Aiken, South Carolina, near the Georgia border. He was exceptionally bright and the first person in his family to attend college and later graduate school. He claimed that he walked seven miles through the woods every day to go to school in a one-room schoolhouse! When my brother, sisters, and I were young, he would tell us repeatedly how important it was for all of us, particularly as African Americans, to be literate. "Boy," he would address me in his gruff voice, "if you can read, write, and count, you can compete!"

On that particular day, he looked at me somberly for a few minutes without saying a word. Fidgeting, I was afraid to say anything because he looked so serious—almost angry. When he finally spoke, he told me that before I ever act in response to something, I must completely understand every aspect of the problem. "If after you have completely grasped this problem, you still choose to fight, then so be it. But first you need to understand why it is you're fighting."

My chin held high, I responded that I was ready to understand the problem. He nodded and said, "There is a book written about everything you will face in life . . . when you face a problem, you should read about it, find out all there is to know about it, then you can act." My father then reached for his bookshelf and gave me several books: *The Autobiography of Malcolm X*, Franz Fanon's *The Wretched of the Earth*, and *The Narrative of the Life of Frederick Douglass: An American Slave*.

This exchange with my father helped me appreciate the need to understand the depths of a problem before lashing out viscerally. By reading the books he offered relating to racism, I gained various perspectives that I would not have seen otherwise. But something more significant resulted from this experience: I developed a thirst for knowledge that could be quenched only through more reading and more education.

One of the most obvious byproducts of racism and segregation has been the lesser status of persons of color in many areas of American life. Usually, the road toward that second-class citizenship begins with a dysfunctional educational experience. The average national graduation rate for the class of 1998 was 74 percent—78 percent for white students, 56 percent for African American students, and 54 percent for Hispanic students.[4] Thurgood Marshall once remarked that without a fair shake at quality education, African Americans would continue to be crippled and forced to run the race of life starting miles behind everyone else.

"The old civil rights movement got us to the lunch counter. The new civil rights agenda is: Can we afford to buy the lunch? And, more importantly, can our kids read the menu?"[5] Equalizing educational opportunities for young people may indeed be our last civil rights challenge. The booming economic conditions of the 1990s served to further divide America into two distinct societies: those who have and those who have not.[6] If we continue along this path, we are bound for a society with a permanent underclass, composed of citizens who are increasingly homeless, jobless, incarcerated, un- or under-educated, and more likely to abuse substances.

Today in our cities, many of our young black men are left to instinctive and often violent reactions in the context of unbearable environmental conditions, never fully appreciating or being exposed to other ways of responding. As a result, not only are we warehousing children through a dysfunctional system, we are also, through benign neglect, creating a permanent underclass, some of whom will become predators who terrorize us.

Given a virtual educational apartheid, African Americans are clamoring for measures to address the education crisis overwhelmingly facing their children.[7] African Americans as a group are far more likely than their white counterparts to support choice in education. A 1999 survey found that 60 percent of blacks—compared to 53 percent of the overall population—support vouchers to help pay for private education. That number increases to 72 percent among blacks earning less than $15,000 a year. These numbers are amazing given that African Americans tend to vote largely Democratic and that school choice—and particularly vouchers—are Republican banner projects.[8,9]

Fixing schools will require radical change and as one education activist has stated, "[W]e must be willing to experiment by any means necessary."[10] The overwhelmingly Democratic District of Columbia residents have exercised choice in large numbers. They have either enrolled their children in private or parochial schools, or simply moved to districts with better-performing schools. Sadly, "[i]t's only poor parents who are left with the ideological privilege of standing by an education system that practically everyone who can afford to has already deserted."[11] Indeed, "Parental school choice is widespread in America—unless you're poor."[12]

The beauty of the charter school movement—especially when drafted and implemented properly with the community in mind and the proper monitoring and oversight measures in place—is that it can help jumpstart reform that takes into account the specialized needs of urban, poor, and special-needs children, a function that the public school system as a whole has been unable to do. Public education is one of society's most important institutions, and if we leave behind a segment of our community, all we are doing is putting ourselves at a disadvantage.

Some theorize that children are often penalized because they can't vote and they are not a natural political constituency. While that may be true, the real fault lies in the inherent inflexibility of the traditional school bureaucracy and the inability of policy makers to allot education reform the needed time and attention to effect necessary change. Nearly every public official or politician who runs for office claims that education is his or her top priority, but in every legislature in the country, just a handful of lawmakers are really involved in this issue. This translates into reality in a negative way and, in a practical sense, makes education reform something less than a priority.

This issue is an even larger problem with today's students than in the past. One of the biggest challenges for those of us involved in education reform is dealing with the socio-economic realities associated with the so-called "haves" and "have-nots" in our society. In the 1990s, the digital age led to an economic boom unparalleled in the history of mankind. We had more millionaires and more citizens entering the upper stratosphere of income levels than ever before. And yet we also had corresponding increases in child poverty, infectious diseases that afflict low-income families, and illiteracy in both urban centers and rural parts of the country. Nowhere is that reality more pronounced than in our schools. My ward happens to include some of the most troubled neighborhoods in Washington, D.C.

Years ago, a person without good reading skills could get a job as a law firm receptionist. With training, this person could develop some typing skills and make a decent living. With the technology explosion of the past decade, it's virtually impossible for an uneducated or undereducated person to get a job even as a receptionist.[13]

What is even more ironic about the reality of the abilities of the average urban student is that the business community is sometimes forced to compensate for this lack of skills in order to have a pool of workers to pick from. One example is fast food restaurants where, because the young people who form their natural employee pool do not have even the most basic skills, the employers have taken to placing pictures of their offerings on the cash registers. Trainees who cannot read are taught to take orders by pushing the button with the appropriate picture on it, and the "smart" cash registers do all the work! Once, during a visit to a local McDonald's, I questioned the change I was given. The young man behind the counter was in such a panic that he had to call the manager. Without the machine, he could not do the very basic math to calculate how much change I should have received.

Many other employers have also "dumbed down" in order to cater to the skill level of their potential employee pool. All of this means that ultimately, if society does not get a handle on its education disparity, many citizens may become permanent members of the underclass and may well end up being completely dependent on, and perhaps even eventually wards of, the state. With the continuing technology advancements, basic skills will become even more necessary. In the District, for example, those working in the welfare-to-work field are finding it harder to bring citizens up to speed because they do not already possess a sound educational foundation.

Giving all children that foundation has become part of our new civil rights challenge. To meet this challenge, we must be open to viable educational alternatives—particularly to reach those children who have been lost in our traditional school system.

CHAPTER 2

Education in the Nation's Capital

"All of life is a constant education."

—Eleanor Roosevelt

The testimony was being taken on the eve of the possible closing of the University of the District of Columbia, a university in the heart of a plush D.C. neighborhood, one ironically attended primarily by students of color, members of the city's working class, and new immigrants. The university was on the verge of closing. There had been several attempts to relocate the university to a less glamorous neighborhood, freeing up its current campus for more lucrative endeavors. Toward the end of the evening, a young woman took the podium. She looked drawn, tired, and slightly disheveled. "I am a single mother," she began quietly. "I work two jobs to support myself and my young son. I never finished high school, but received my diploma last year after attending night school. I now attend UDC. Sometimes I come here at nights after a ten-hour workday. Sometimes I have to bring my son to school because I can't find someone to watch him. I spend almost an hour on the bus and the metro to get here, and the same to get back. I struggle to get here and struggle to stay in school. And sometimes I cry on the bus because it's so hard to stay in school. I used to hide my tears from my son. Now I don't. And I'm glad. I'm glad that my son gets to see me struggle to finish my education. You know why? Because I want him to know the value of an education. I want him to be willing to struggle, if he has to, to get his own. I want him to walk through this neighborhood and see the possibilities for his future. Please do not close down this school."

When I ran for public office initially, I did not do so with the idea of fixing schools. My entrance into local politics was probably similar to that of most people. You run to make a difference. I felt that I could make the most difference in local government through efficient city services and economic development in concert with neighborhood interests. Even now as I talk to fellow legislators around the country, it is noteworthy how few are drawn to running for public office because they want to reform education. We all say education is a number one priority, but historically that is not why most people seek public office.

After several years on the city council, my perspective has evolved to the point that education reform and equal access to quality education have become a passion. Because education reform is so difficult and the political downsides so acute, it's not the most attractive area in which to stake your political future. But more elected officials need to be attuned to the nuances of this issue. Mayors in New York, Detroit, Chicago, D.C., and Milwaukee have all reached the point where they recognize that if you do not fix public education, you will be promoting the cycle of poverty, despair, and illiteracy which ultimately leads to urban decay, because neighborhoods end up reflecting the social conditions around them.

I became involved in politics in the late 1980s when members of the River Terrace community, the Northeast Washington ward I was living in, asked me to help them fight against Potomac Electric Power Company (Pepco), our local electric company. At the time, I was a young lawyer and word got out that I had volunteered to help rewrite some bylaws for various civic associations. Pepco had decided to expand its power plant by building two new generators in the heart of my predominantly black neighborhood, which would have increased the pollution output in the community, which was already suffering from its proximity to the city incinerator and a nearby freeway. Community members had launched a series of protests, feeling that it was a classic case of environmental racism, exercised routinely in other cities where corporate polluters often chose the path of least resistance by locating in areas where they felt they would face minimal opposition.

When the community members called on me, they were desperate and felt that the city leadership was not working with them. I took on the case against our local utility, and we won! Pepco—which had spent millions putting combustion turbine engines at the plant—had to scrap its plans. We held a neighborhood rally on Earth Day, with Jesse Jackson, Greenpeace, and the Sierra Club headlining demonstrations.

This case served as my entrée to community service. After I had a taste of being involved at that level, I saw that there were many more social service needs. I decided to run for office to make a difference and to make sure that more resources would come to the community.

Within my first three to four years on the D.C. council, I came to grips with the overwhelming aspects of trying to provide egalitarian services to a long-neglected community. Similar to my later experience in dealing with schools, I thought the problem of disparity could be solved by additional financial resources and commitments. However, while there is some truth to that, there also has to be a systemic reordering of priorities and focus on changing the long-entrenched culture of neglect. The old expression about teaching people how to fish, rather than giving them a fish, holds true in this area.

Unfortunately, many who have not been offered the tools

to do for themselves develop a dependency mindset. They expect everything to be done for them. With schools, many community members just trust schools to do what they are supposed to be doing. Whole generations of families do not have the wherewithal to navigate bureaucracies for themselves. We need to focus on educating people across the board, not just in terms of reading, writing, and counting, but in terms of making decisions for themselves. That's why the whole community outreach aspect of education is so critical in schools and various other aspects of social services.

Once I began focusing on education as Education Committee chairman, it did not take long for me to establish equal access to a quality education as my number one priority. Now, equal access to quality education is enormously difficult to execute. For many children who come from solid two-parent households that take an interest in their education, the goal of equal access is far more attainable. But in many of the communities I represent in Southeast and Northeast Washington, east of the Anacostia River, the circumstances are far more complex. My visits to schools in my ward and my conversations with parents, teachers, and community activists enhanced my understanding of the disparities of public education, particularly urban public education systems.

The D.C. experience represents an example of both the good and bad in traditional public education. Forty years ago, the District had a two-tiered education system based on race. Some schools were designated for black children and others for whites. In both of these systems, D.C. used the "tracking system" to educate children. Tracking involves dividing children into four different groups, according to aptitude. Group 1 was the honors track for gifted children. Group 2 included the next brightest, including those children who were on the college preparatory track. Group 3, which was essentially the vocational track, served the bulk of students. Finally, group 4 was considered the "dumb" group, consisting of those children who were described as slow learners.[14]

This led to amazing disparities in educational opportunities for children who happened to be going to black schools and for those in groups 3 and 4. In effect, you had a separate system in D.C. based on race and another based on each child's perceived academic proficiency. The tracking started in first grade, and the end result was that children who were in the slow group in the first grade were doomed to be in that group for their entire tenure in school, missing out on key academic components geared for the other, more "intelligent" children.

This system was put in place and preserved by Congress through the commissioner form of government.[15] One by-product of the 1960s civil rights movement was the escalating demand for D.C. home rule with advocates fighting for voting rights and equal representation for the District so that it could be treated like every other jurisdiction. (If you've visited the District in the past few years, you may have seen our license plates that decry "Taxation Without Representation.") The advocates used the schools as a focal point for their cause. While they were lobbying on Capitol Hill for voting rights, they would point to the schools' tracking system and segregation as examples of how black children were not being educated properly.

As a compromise in the late 1960s, the president and Congress agreed to allow District citizens to elect their own school board. The school board would, in turn, select a superintendent to run the schools. This took place in 1971 and was the first instance of home rule for the city. Later in 1974, Congress and the president gave the District home rule as we now know it, permitting District citizens to elect the mayor and a thirteen-member city council that, theoretically, would run the government. There were several provisos, of course, including Congress's ability to overturn these bills if they were found to impact federal interest and also congressional oversight of the city's budget.

Election of school board members in 1971 represented the first time in history that District residents voted on local officials. Because of this, the school board has always had a special significance for D.C. residents. Many home-rule advocates—Julius Hobson, Hilda Mason, and Marion Barry— were elected to that first school board. What District residents did not appreciate at the time, but has become painfully clear in retrospect, is that the political overlay associated with the school board being the first elected position in the city in effect overpoliticized our schools.

For the twenty-five-year period from 1971 to 1995, a large number of school board members came and went. Many of them did not really want to be on the school board, but saw the board as an entry point for political office. The school board became their platform for other ambitions of either running for the D.C. Council or for Mayor, as opposed to seeing the school board as a commitment to ensuring that District children were receiving a quality education. This was, in fact, the path that Marion Barry, who was eventually elected mayor, took. As a result, children's interests often became secondary to what would advance the political interests of board members.

In 1992, when I decided to run for city council, many friends and advisors told me to run for the school board first to "get my name out there." But I had no desire to serve on the school board—I wanted to be on the city council! And yet so many other city politicians and council members went the school board route first. Some were successful, others not.

The overpoliticization of the school system started the moment District residents got the ability to elect school board members. And the politics on the board began with the selection of the superintendent. Whenever a new superintendent was hired, it was understood that he or she would have to do political favors for board members whose political aspirations and path had been calculated far in advance. Complicating this web of special interests was that Congress had provided the elected school board with an authority no other board in the country had: the ability to sign off on every hire made by the superintendent. The school board had the right to approve every position from custodian to principal. What ensued were circumstances where board members would play politics with individual schools: I will scratch your back now if you scratch mine later.

In most other jurisdictions, the board sets general policy and hires a superintendent who makes decisions on specific matters such as personnel, construction, and procurement, among others. D.C.'s board, in contrast, got involved in virtually every nitty-gritty detail. In many ways, this compromised the authority of the superintendents. Early on, the District had some great superintendents like Vincent Reed and Floretta McKenzie, who were excellent by all measures. Part of their success was their ability to maneuver through the politics of the school board.

The school system did well during the late 1970s and early 1980s, but then politics took hold and more board members came in with political aspirations. They would take actions such as steering contracts toward potential political allies and friends who, for example, claimed to have a construction business but clearly knew nothing about patching roofs. Some board members would cut deals with an incoming superintendent: You hire this principal and I will approve your appointment. And those board members' deal making continued once the principal was in place. In the 1980s, you could look through the school system's list of employees and find scores of employees with the same surnames as board members: a custodian here, a teacher there, an administrator elsewhere. This, along with other factors, eventually led to the complete and utter deterioration of the D.C. public school system.

It is now well known that in 1994, after Marion Barry was reelected, the city was discovered to have a $500 million deficit, compelling Congress to establish a control board to oversee the city's finances and theoretically to work on reform.[16] One of the control board's first orders of business was an intense review of the public schools. Among other findings, the evaluation noted that cronyism engulfed the system, test scores were among the lowest in the country, the facilities were in shambles, and the children were not learning. The control board stripped the elected school board of its powers and appointed an emergency board of trustees to run the schools.[17]

The control board wanted to show that it was serious about making a difference, and that is why it focused on schools. Along with the city's deficit, the schools were the most obvious examples of the District's failures. At one point, it seemed that every week brought a new story highlighting the schools' fiascoes. One such debacle was the Service Master contract, a multi-million dollar contract for the maintenance of schools, which had been steered to a school board member's friend—with disastrous results. The front page of the Washington Post highlighted in embarrassing detail what the city was paying for maintenance, and how that maintenance was not being done. Later, the city was overwhelmed with constant stories about leaking roofs and dilapidated classrooms.

Parents, schools, and advocacy groups united to sue the school system over inadequate facilities, which led to a local judge riding herd on the situation. The first day of school had to be postponed for several weeks. The control board made a strategic decision to show that it was serious about reform. It appointed a retired black Army general, Julius Becton, to run the schools. He, in turn, brought in the U.S. Army Corps of Engineers to handle all school repairs and maintenance.

I became chairman of the education committee right after the control board took over and appointed Becton. My frustration with the control board stemmed from their insistence on reform taking place from the top down. And if I learned anything from the experience of working with that group of well-intentioned, honorable, and well-respected business and civil leaders in the community is that your status and stature alone mean nothing if you are trying to reform public education. Public education can work only when you involve the community that is supposed to benefit from your reform efforts. As we now know from our experience with many successful charter schools, an entire community must be invested in children's schooling.

The control board made the mistake of securing education experts—many ivy-league educated—who were not from the District, placing them in key positions, and expecting the community to be grateful that these "experts" were coming in to save their schools. The problem with that in an urban setting is that a lot of these new folks did not even know their way around the city. They were not cognizant of the social conditions that the children brought to school with them, and they did not know where to go and who to talk to in dealing with those conditions. They knew little about engaging the community, and in particular, the parents and the kids. That led to the implementation of reform efforts that were later rejected at the community level.

One positive outcome of the control board's tenure was the inauguration of the charter school movement in the District. In 1996, the council and Congress both passed charter school legislation. A year later, we still had no charter schools or funding for them, so we set out to integrate charters into the public's mindset and to carve out a budget for them. We held numerous public hearings and asked both the charter school board (the federal body that authorizes charters) and the board of education (the local District of Columbia body that authorizes charters) to help educate the public about charter schools.[18] By then, charter advocates had begun to start up some schools and apply for charters. Edison Schools was one of the first to apply,[19] followed quickly by several others.

I first began regularly visiting schools in early 1997 just as the control board took over. The District had pending lawsuits about leaky roofs and other maintenance issues, and it was apparent that our schools were physically in shambles. In several buildings, first and second graders had to wear coats inside the classroom because it was so cold. Other elementary-school children literally had to hold buckets during class to catch the water leaking from the ceiling. In some schools, children were designated to take turns in dumping the buckets. These were conditions similar to those of developing countries.

I found it interesting that most children and teachers were very accepting of these negative conditions. They did not complain much and had grown accustomed to doing what they had to do to learn around the adverse conditions. When they did complain, it was mostly about the food. Many of the children in my ward live below the poverty line, and for some of these children, the best meal of the day is the one they receive during school. The contractors who ran the school lunch program were terrible. They served prepackaged food, some of it moldy, most of it barely edible. Everywhere I went, teachers, principals, and students virtually begged me to fix the food situation.

The control board's appointee, General Becton, had hired his army colleague, General Charles Williams, to run the facilities, and he was also given responsibility for the food service. Williams vowed to fix the food service shortcomings. To this day, I am convinced that Williams did not talk to parents or students about the problem. Instead, he came to an agreement with a contractor, and convinced that he had resolved the food issue, publicly uttered words he would later regret: "This food is so good, you could serve it for Sunday dinner." The complaints escalated tenfold.

On one occasion, I decided to take local television cameras along on visits to three different schools. I sat down with children from elementary, junior high, and middle schools for lunch. The food was so atrocious that some of the children whose parents could not afford to feed them refused to eat. Parents on public assistance explained that they were piecing together lunches because their children were going hungry in school. At the time, Arlene Ackerman had been brought in from Seattle to serve as deputy superintendent for academic affairs, with the understanding that she would eventually be promoted to superintendent. She and I talked and agreed on a solution to the food issue: Instead of trying to negotiate with the food contractor again as General Williams had, we set up a committee that included staff from both of our offices, as well as teachers, parents, and several high-school students.

For several months, the committee conducted research and consulted on its findings. Students testified in hearings before the city council. After deliberations, the committee chose a new contractor that it felt would better meet the needs of its elementary and middle schools. The high schools instituted a food court concept. The number of food complaints have dwindled to a handful per year—compared to thousands over the same period in previous years.

The federal control board was officially disbanded in 2000 and the trustees' power reverted back to the elected school board. In 1999, in anticipation of this event, I introduced legislation redefining the school board's roles and responsibilities, ensuring that we would not go back to the way things had been. I felt that the biggest problem with the school board was not that the members were elected, but that they had too much power to interfere on minute levels. Changing and clarifying the board members' role was a key step to reform.

They were to be a policy-making board like others around the country, with no authority in day-to-day management, steering contracts, and school-level decision making. The legislation reduced the size of the elected board from eleven to nine members because studies showed that smaller boards work better. Although most of my colleagues supported the legislation, I caught a lot of heat. The mayor had his own plans for the board: The board members' roles and responsibilities would remain as redefined by the legislation, but the Mayor wanted to take over the schools. He wanted a five-member school board—all appointed by him.

A big fight ensued between the council and the mayor, and ultimately a compromise emerged whereby there would be a hybrid school board of five elected members and four members appointed by the mayor and confirmed by the council. Since all of this required a change in the city's charter, it was taken to a referendum before the public, and in May 2000 the voters narrowly approved it. The new approach is better than what was in place prior to the control board, mainly because the school board members' roles are better defined. The superintendent now has more managerial power. Today the hybrid board and Superintendent Vance are working hard to reform D.C. Public Schools (DCPS). Some board members do not realize, however, how intractable the school bureaucracy is. We are still a long way from true reform. And the hybrid board is often resistant to new ways of doing business. For example, the board has not embraced charters—even those charter schools that the board itself has authorized. While many board members realize that some of the good programs in selected charter schools are worthy of replication in our traditional school system, some members remain parochial and protective of the school bureaucracy's status quo.[20]

CHAPTER 3

Using the Community as the Hub

"Parents have become so convinced educators know what is best for children that they forget that they themselves are really the experts."

—Marian Wright Edelman

Principal Linda McKay was assigned to the Patricia Roberts Harris School in May 1992. Located in a high-crime neighborhood composed predominantly of low-income residents, the school housed eleven hundred students from pre-K to grade nine—85 percent of them receiving free or reduced-price lunch.

When McKay joined the Harris School, the community was at the height of a crisis, with drastically increased drug activity in the neighborhood and large numbers of both students and parents using drugs. In McKay's first month, a security guard was shot on the school grounds—the first such incident in the country. During her first year, there were several deaths around the school, in the playground, and directly across the street. One particular raid unearthed nine guns in the school building.

Wracked by violence, the school's atmosphere was highly charged. Many of McKay's young students were under an immense amount of pressure, both in school and at home. McKay, who had begun as principal of the elementary division and in November 1994 took over as interim principal, knew something more comprehensive had to be done for her children aside from their academic needs. She also knew she couldn't do it by herself.

During 1994 the school had hosted Turning Points, a targeted program providing social and wraparound services for the children. But in the face of the mounting city deficit, the Mayor had decided that the program would be cut for the following year. Expecting that her already crippled school would be hit hard by the funding and program cuts, McKay sprang into action.

Linda McKay is an elegant woman, with short-cropped hair, caramel skin, and bright eyes. But her calm, even-tempered exterior belies the steely resolve beneath. In an impassioned plea before the City Council, she presented them with two options: You invest in my children now while they are in school or you invest in them later when they are in jail.

This message was delivered before a packed room stunned into silence by the import of her words. Struck by McKay's poignant arguments, Councilmember William Lightfoot requested that he and McKay continue the discussion after the hearing.

In the subsequent days, McKay and Lightfoot tried to figure out how to provide services to the students and save money. They set out to bring existing city services into the Harris school building. Including the school superintendent and mayor in their discussions, they began a citywide joint initiative to provide wraparound services[21] not just for Harris students but also for the surrounding community. Everyone brought in to work with the students—social, mental, and health service providers—also worked with the students' families. The ultimate objective: helping students perform academically.

The partnership was effective beyond their wildest dreams. McKay and her coworkers were able to bring so much to the students—not just with city agencies but also with private partnerships. The city helped with recreation activities. Probation officers came to the school. Police officers visited and talked to the students about truancy. The Department of Employment Services came and provided job training. Harris received funding for band and other arts programs. At one point, McKay offered the school building to an organization looking for a place to do Internet training. As a result, the Harris school was networked for free. Consultants were brought in to train teachers and students to develop web pages. The students, in turn, trained their parents in the skills they had just learned. Community members were trained in child development, nutrition, and parenting skills. Faith-based organizations were brought in to do their part.

That year, Patricia Roberts Harris School was a vibrant place. On any given night, the school's doors were open until 9:00 P.M. "Midnight basketball" was offered. The school PTA grew from ten people to PTA meetings of a hundred or more. Academics improved in the school, and violence decreased in both the school and the community. Linda McKay had, in fact, created a community hub in the Patricia Roberts Harris School.

If you ask Linda McKay, she will point to one major reason why the program did not last: the bureaucracy of the traditional system. Some did not like all the hoopla surrounding the Harris program. They saw it as unnecessary because it wasn't purely academic. They did not realize that it was okay for value to leave the school and go into the home.

Others thought the Harris program was a great idea. So great, in fact, that they tried to appropriate it for nearby schools of their choice. McKay, who is now involved in the charter school movement, notes that if there is a good idea in a charter school, it cannot be killed by what another charter school wants to do. In the public school system, however, when people see something that works, they want it! And that's understandable. The problem is that an approach cannot be arbitrarily taken from one school and dropped into another without adequate leadership, preparation, and context. The right forces must be in place to support the initiative. Otherwise it withers and dies.

In the end, the Patricia Roberts Harris program buckled under the pressure of turf wars.

Reflecting back, a wistful McKay doubts that the Harris School experience could happen again in the traditional school system—not unless the right leadership and the right forces were in place:

> The program has to come from the heart. It can't be someone coming in and enforcing a program without context. We had a City Council that listened to the call for what we needed for our schools. We had school administrators who were prepared to give us the autonomy we wanted. We had teachers who would bring me ideas that they thought might work; who were willing to stay as late as they needed to in order to help their students. We had happier children and a different community. We had mental health services with open doors. What we had could not be replicated in the bureaucracy again.
>
> It was, after all, a one-moment-in-time type of a thing.

In urban America, the community hub concept is becoming increasingly popular and essential due to the dysfunctions present in some poor home settings.[22] These dysfunctions demand flexibility within the system and autonomy on the part of the school to meet varying needs in different communities. The community hub concept holds that by using public schools as a center, many partners, including families, local government and business, and other organizations can come together to provide support and opportunities for the community's children, their families, and the community itself, serving educational, social, cultural, and recreational needs. Most community hub schools are open long before and after regular schools, seven days a week. Because of the close relationship between the school and the community's families, hub schools can even serve as a needs assessment for the well-being and development of the community at large.

Many charter schools operate from the premise that parents bear the ultimate responsibility for their children's education, and that a school should be both a community unto itself and an interactive component of the larger community in which it exists. A school founded on the community hub principle serves as an anchor for its community and seeks to support holistic student achievement—not just academically—through the use of family and youth services, adult education, parent academies, and crime prevention.[23]

On a macro level in the District, the community hub schools represent a collaborative effort between the Executive Office of the Mayor, the D.C. Council and the D.C. Public Schools. They require agency support from the Department of Recreation and Parks, the Department of Human Services, the Commission of Public Health, the Metropolitan Police Department, the Superior Court of the District of Columbia, and the Department of Employment Services. Often, private partnerships are necessary with satellite mental health providers, private practice physicians and dentists, faith-based programs, individual tutors, and even banks to support student banking programs.

Most community hub schools do not have a single funding source. Faced with the difficult challenge of raising funds for the operation of core school functions, community schools often turn to sources as diverse as corporations; foundations; federal, state, or local governments; local businesses; and individuals. To illustrate, funding sources for Linda McKay's community hub efforts included enterprise school grants of up to $30,000 to schools for autonomous spending; city services and D.C. agency employees redirected to Patricia Roberts Harris's Education Center; Title funding—federal supplemental funding to augment and support school-wide student achievement programs; and in-kind services.

Many of the charter schools featured in this book are actively engaged in developing a "hub school model" to gather community resources in collaboration with social services, health services, and academic and corporate partners to help children succeed in school and later in life.

Linda McKay's experiment at the Harris School worked because good, caring teachers wanted to help meet their students' needs and were allowed to teach beyond the nine-to-three model. Social services, employment services, the health agency, police and fire departments, private-sector representatives—all were committed to following the guidance and direction of Linda McKay to provide resources not just for the school's children but also for their families who were in need of particular assistance. And so much of what they were able to accomplish by bringing all those entities into the building and coordinating their interaction and activities with parents and families went beyond what the traditional bureaucracy is usually able to absorb.

The various government agencies involved at the school were not focused on who was getting credit or who was controlling the outreach. They were not focused on whether their budget would have to absorb more than another agency's budget to make this experiment work. They were not focused on putting the paperwork associated with doing the job ahead of doing the job itself. Rather, the sole focus was on making sure that the students' and community's needs were met. They designed an approach tailored to the community's interests, as opposed to trying to force the community's interests into a traditional approach that might or might not work.

For all its success, the inherent nature of the bureaucracy eventually killed the community hub concept at the Harris School. As McKay notes, because they were having success, the respective agency executives away from the school wanted to exert increasing control over the school's day-to-day activities. The bureaucratic chiefs wanted credit for certain successes and pointed fingers at other agencies whenever something went wrong. Battles over budget allocations and who would pay for what aspect of which service began to get in the way of the school's early success. It became clear to McKay that what they were attempting to do at the Harris School was so unique, innovative, and nontraditional that it worked only because certain supportive forces came together at the right time. But even Linda McKay came to see the near impossibility of maintaining the community hub concept in the traditional school bureaucracy.

By comparison, charters offer policy makers the opportunity to provide innovations like the community hub concept without bureaucratic interference. One of the closest examples of a charter school in D.C. using an approach similar to that of McKay at the Harris School is the Community Academy Public Charter School, founded by Kent Amos. As with the Harris School in the mid-1990s, one can walk into the Community Academy building at 6:00 or 7:00 P.M. to find the school as vibrant, active, and engaged in offering a variety of activities as if it were 11:00 A.M. Just as important, after school hours one sees large numbers of parents and community residents taking GED courses, attending PTA meetings, and helping kids with homework. This approach can be maintained and sustained because once the resources enter a particular charter school, they will remain there as long as they are needed. In other words, teachers and principals at a community academy do not have to worry about the "folks downtown" pulling the plug on something that's working.

Charter schools are not necessarily community schools, and that is why there's utility in the charter school concept—because not every charter school should be a community hub. One size does not fit all, so the flexibility and autonomy allow a wide range of charters offering numerous approaches to educating children. This approach is difficult, if not impossible, to achieve in traditional school systems.[24]

CHAPTER 4

Problems in
Public Education

"The only person who is educated is the one who has learned
how to learn and change."

—Carl Rogers

Late one afternoon I received an urgent call at my home
from a local high school teacher. Could I come right away? I
said that I would, grabbed a member of my staff and headed
over to the school. The teacher was waiting in front of the
school for me. He took me inside and showed me a crawl
space in the roof. Beyond this crawl space was where one of
the students had been living for almost a year. The boy was
seventeen years old and a senior. Neither of his parents was
around. He had been living in a foster home when he began
having problems with his foster parents.

The teacher explained that initially he had thought it
strange that the child was always around for all the evening
activities. He came to every meeting and every practice for
every club! One day, the curious teacher followed the boy as
he went upstairs and through a hole in the wall. In a small
room in the school attic, the child had set up a cot, his
clothes, and his toothbrush. He would shower in the boys'
locker room early in the morning.

When he was finally caught, the boy's greatest fear was

that he wouldn't be permitted to finish his senior year. Recognizing that his foster care experience had been less than satisfactory, we found this child a place to stay to finish out the school year. I believe that when he turned eighteen, he joined the military.

This incident provides a context for understanding the depth of the problems in some of our communities. While I am not suggesting that charter schools can or will solve all these problems, it is these types of desperate situations that our children face daily and which require a certain amount of flexibility and creativity that traditional schools are either unwilling or unable to apply.

The long-ailing American public education system has proven itself largely ineffective and incapable of serving students with diverse needs. Poor schools hurt children and stifle their potential. Students at either end of the spectrum—those who are particularly bright, or in need of dramatic remedial help—tend to fall through the cracks in public schools. Some students may need extra time, tutoring, or assessment, but most traditional schools are either unable or unwilling to give it to them. Yet other children may need more than academic assistance, but this need, too, is not met. The failure to meet needs creates a cycle of despair in almost all education stakeholders, particularly the student.

It is an oft-repeated truth that it takes a village to raise a child. Failure to invest in our most vulnerable children has ramifications for the entire society: For example, in the District of Columbia Public Schools, of the 4,935 eighth graders in 1993–94, only 2,777 earned high school diplomas in 1998.[25] The rest were incarcerated, lost to substance abuse or violent crimes, or went on to some other nonproductive lifestyle. Research suggests that investing more in education services for disadvantaged students can help close the achievement gap. Investing in our children can result in increased student achievement, increased attendance, increased parent involvement, extended school hours, community building, student talent development, technology development, tutorials, and mental health services for families.[26]

Unfortunately, most public school districts have not shown themselves capable of the flexibility, creativity, or foresight necessary to provide children with appropriate interventions. Schools' inflexibility and one-size-fits-all approach leaves large numbers of students in the cold, and prevents the schools from developing rewarding private-sector and other partnerships or serving anyone outside their immediate radius.

Of course, the one-size-fits-all approach to public education is flawed. We cannot expect all children to enter the schoolhouse door the way they did in the 1940s, '50s, and '60s. Nearly every teacher I know agonizes over those two or three children in the classroom who come from totally dysfunctional home circumstances. Teachers struggle daily with how to compensate for what those children are not receiving at home. In many frustrating scenarios, it is often those same two or three children who disrupt entire classrooms and thwart learning for the entire class. It becomes virtually impossible for any of the children to learn unless the needs of the few "problem" children are addressed.

Too many urban children hail from dysfunctional and toxic family environments; thus it is essential to develop a direct collaborative relationship between the school system and government social services agencies. Every child should be in a pre-K program at age three; health assessments should be done for all children before first grade; cognitive determinations and environmental status should be reviewed before a child enters first grade to allow the school system to determine what support is needed outside the school day, if anything. Most traditional schools are simply not used to operating that way.

I was introduced to books by a father who understood and valued books and education, who pushed me and made it feasible for me to do what I wanted to do in life. Many

American children will never have the privilege of that type of parental influence, but society has an obligation to children in need. Like most Americans, I am a strong believer in adhering to a core curriculum that will provide every child with a baseline education, but the context in which that education is provided has to be malleable enough so that other, related public services can aid and motivate children. I recognize that principals and teachers can't supplant parents. However, a full complement of wraparound services working with human services and other agencies to support children and their families can be provided at each school. Where needed, children must have access to and be able to benefit from longer school years and days and more rigorous curricula introduced at a younger age.

Overwhelming Bureaucracy

Years ago, I believed that the inherent disparities in the system could be addressed economically. That is, if we could give schools in low-performing areas more money and resources, that would make the difference between achievement and failure. So, in my first few years as Education Committee chairman, I was on a mission to increase funding across the board for our schools and to put into place a system that would ensure that more of our needy schools would receive the resources they deserved. What I discovered was that when you provide funds to a traditional school district, there are too many hands that money must pass through. The bureaucracy gobbles it up!

This would be vastly different if true local school autonomy existed. From 1999 to 2003, the mayor and City Council allocated 300 million new dollars for public schools, a 41 percent increase in the schools' budget. During that same period, traditional schools' overall student population decreased by over ten thousand students. We have 146 schools in our traditional system, and many of these schools individually can do great things with their allotments based on their student populations. But when this new money is received by the school system, it does not seem to filter down to the classroom level, as hard as we may fight for that to happen.

I came to this realization when I was campaigning for reelection in 2000. I would attend debates and public forums, and in my opening remarks, I would list all the things I was proud of. I would lead with reciting what I had done in education reform, how I had helped develop charter schools in the District, how I was in the forefront of ensuring that the traditional schools received more resources.

Every time I mentioned these points in front of groups from my ward, I saw blank faces and little or no positive reaction from my constituents. Finally, during one debate, an older woman raised her hand and said: "Councilmember, if you were able to get all that money for the school system, how come I don't see any difference in my grandson's classroom?" The reality of the situation hit me like a ten-ton truck. Why isn't all the money we are allocating to our schools translating into a higher quality education for our children?

Visiting traditional public schools even as recently as 2002, when we added another $90 million to the school budget, I was baffled to hear how often principals and teachers talk about having to spend their own money for the most basic supplies—toilet paper, pencils, books. This is something I never hear when I visit charters. So the real question here is: What happens to the money? The existing school infrastructure works hard to maintain itself and the status quo—that is, the salaries of the assistant to the assistant to the assistant and the contracts for the brother and sister-in-law of the assistant! It becomes a quagmire, ensuring that resources do not flow to the classroom. Compare this to the lean bureaucracy of Catholic schools. Catholic schools work because they believe both in discipline and in tailoring schools to the needs of the community they serve. They also strongly believe in minimizing input from their central administration. There are seven directors out of a total of eleven employees (including support staff) running 110 Catholic schools in the central administration office of the Washington Metropolitan Archdiocese. This office's public school counterpart has over 1,500 staff members, under dozens of subdivisions, running 146 schools.

When Dr. Paul Vance was first appointed D.C. Public School Superintendent, he stated that the problem in the District was not one of money or resources. He eventually backed away from that statement because a natural law of the universe dictates that all superintendents would like as much money allocation as they can get! However, it is clear that when a system is broken and basic competence is lacking in many key areas, you pay more for what you need to compensate for ineffectiveness and dead weight. The D.C. Superintendent acknowledged that a fair amount of dead weight is restraining the school bureaucracy, and resources that could be flowing to the children are blocked elsewhere instead.

Traditional public school principals and teachers often complain that in some circumstances, despite urgency and the need to move swiftly, their hands are tied because of bureaucratic rules that must be followed. For example, part of the central administration's job is to interact with the police. The social services agency has several units that may intervene, given various specific scenarios. In some instances, legal counsel for the school system must be involved. It is understandable that sometimes administrative and bureaucratic rules must exist. At the same time, many individual charter, private, and parochial schools—operating without those shackles—operate far more effectively to help children. The bureaucracy in a traditional public school protects itself fiercely whereas with a charter, the school and the community have a single focus and interest: What's going on in that school?

In 2002, the school system sent Reduction in Force notices (also known as RIFs) to 1,100 central school administration employees, asking these workers essentially to reapply for their jobs. Some of these employees were effectively categorized as central administration staff, but were actually school-based personnel.

Unfortunately, some who lost their jobs should not have been the ones losing them. The real focus should have been placed on the teachers, former principals, and administrators who had problems in a school and were pushed out. These employees were then detailed to central administration where a spot was created for them because the school bureaucracy has a way of taking care of its own. Even in a RIF scenario, however, these same employees are the last to go because of the relationships they have with the bureaucracy's leadership—those who hold positions of influence, such as the chief academic officers and heads of facilities. Many education bureaucracy leaders started as teachers themselves, alongside these protected employees. Are you more likely to cut someone who started in education with you twenty-five years ago, or some custodian who was detailed to a random school across town? The sad reality is that the truly dispensable employees often find allies to help them keep their jobs.

I absolutely believe in creating a competitive atmosphere that will drive the central administration to cut its bloat. We must squeeze the life out of the superfluous aspects of the bureaucracy by applying pressure from both ends: from the top, by creating more schooling options and tying funding to enrollments, thereby eventually distributing fewer dollars to an ineffective system; and from the bottom, by encouraging greater local autonomy in traditional public schools. The single most effective means of reform is getting rid of education's central bureaucracy by reducing administration in the central school system and empowering local principals.

This is easier said than done, of course, and will take years. But competition from alternative schools helps even with that, and that is what we are seeing in the District. The traditional school system is beginning to see charter schools' steady traction in the District. This traction has served to create a more dramatic sense of urgency among traditional school administrators. That urgency becomes even more significant as the mayor and city council continue to fund schools on a per-pupil basis.

Lack of Coordination among Schools, Social Services, and Other Agencies

One year I attended a Christmas party hosted by a local bank and attended by retired members of the Washington Redskins, local officials, and the press. Bank officials had invited members of a sixth-grade class from my ward to the party. This particular school was from one of the lowest-income communities in the city. The children were to be presented with the only Christmas gifts they were likely to receive that year.

As the gifts were distributed and we watched the children run around with their new toys, I was struck by a young man who was exhibiting a lot of leadership. He was organizing where the children would sit and taking cues from the teacher to make sure that the children did not open their gifts before they were supposed to. I could not take my eyes off this child who seemed to be a natural-born leader. I made a comment to that effect to the boy's teacher.

"Yes," the teacher replied, "he is one of my brightest and most promising. I just hope he makes it." Taken aback, I asked what she meant. She explained that for the first few weeks of school, the little boy was always prepared, ready with his homework, and eager to volunteer answers in class. He then began falling asleep in class on a regular basis. Irritated, the teacher chastised him and asked him to set an example for the rest of the class.

"But it just kept happening and I couldn't understand the sudden change. Finally I decided to do some investigating. This eleven-year-old child lived at home with his mother.

His father was in jail, and his mother was on crack. He also had a six-year-old brother at home. Every day he would rush home with his brother, help him with his homework, cook dinner, and quickly put his brother to bed and close the door to the bedroom before the mother woke up for her nightly binge. The mother was sleeping during the day and using drugs all night. When she would wake up in the early evening, the child would give his mother dinner and then try to get out of her way. Her friends would show up every night around the same time. This child would sit on the stoop waiting for them to leave before he could go to bed. He was up half the night until his mother and her friends fell into a crack-induced sleep. I'm guessing he was going on about two to three hours of sleep a night."

Along with many of my Council colleagues,[27] I have long advocated for better coordination between the traditional school system and our city's social services agencies. It is only when children are nourished, encouraged, and properly cared for that they are ready to learn. While it seems obvious that this coordination should occur, in most places, sadly, it does not. Control over turf and budget has been a big barrier to this needed collaboration. The barrier can be broken, however, through innovative and creative integration of children's social services needs with their educational needs. For this to happen, state and local officials must be willing and committed to forcing collaboration. That task is nearly impossible to accomplish in the traditional bureaucracy-laden school district.

In most jurisdictions, school districts, school management, and social services are separate and independent areas. Generally, a school district is responsible for direct public education of children, and social services is responsible for setting and managing policy in the health department, managing public-assistance dollars and other federal subsidies for lower-income families, dealing with juvenile delinquents and foster children, and meeting the social service needs of citizens—from meals on wheels to prenatal care.

Social service programs often run the gamut. Those two traditionally distinct areas intersect with increasing frequency because of dysfunctional home settings.

However, school systems and social services agencies do not always collaborate or even coordinate their intervention activities. In the District, for example, I have seen, with disturbing frequency, instances where a teacher expresses concern about a child who regularly comes to school battered and bruised. Under such circumstances, teachers are responsible for alerting the principal and contacting the police. The police, in turn, contact the social services agency, which conducts a home study to determine whether the child should be removed. After all that happens, a court proceeding allows the family the opportunity to explain its circumstances. If the court finds fault on the part of the parents, it orders counseling and, in extreme cases, removes the child from the home and places him or her in foster care or with relatives.

In one instance, a teacher pointed out a child who had begun exhibiting extreme behavioral problems. The teacher, along with the principal, called the police, and the child was removed from the classroom for several days while a home study was conducted. Eventually, social services agreed that with counseling, the child's interests would be best served with the parent. Soon after, the child returned to the school once again beaten and bruised. The teacher called me in frustration because she had to go through the social services process all over again—with very little consequence, she felt. She expressed her frustration about social workers who seem intent on preserving the status quo—often to the child's detriment.

There are many instances where better coordination between those two agencies and a primary focus on the child's interest is warranted. The turf battle comes into play when social services representatives try to limit their participation to a discreet function and refuse to do anything beyond that. It is difficult for children to be shuttled back and forth between different social services representatives. And to already overwhelmed social services personnel, once a file is passed on, it is out of sight, out of mind.

In order to determine who is in the best position to address children's needs, we must go back to the community hub concept, undertaking a holistic approach to dealing with a child's needs. The first line of defense for at-risk children will always be teachers and then principals. In turn, schools need to develop a solid collaborative relationship with human and social services agencies and with the health department. In my view, children should enter a certified pre-K program at three years of age. Over the next two years, while in that program, children may be assessed with respect to their cognitive abilities, the state of their health (e.g., whether they've been fully immunized), and their home and social environments. Where there are problems, specific interventions can take place long before the children are well down the road to a potentially negative educational experience. An instruction and outreach plan can be developed for each child that is compatible with his or her needs—one that is designed to maximize learning potentials.

Other Vested Interests

An additional problem with traditional schools is that they no longer look at the output for their children as the top priority. Having been called "as powerful a monopoly as has ever existed,"[28] the American education system often seems principally focused on the output for its employees—clearly a misplaced concentration. According to Al Shanker, the American Federation of Teachers' legendary first president, "It's time to admit that public education operates like a planned economy, a bureaucratic system in which everyone's role is spelled out in advance, and there are few incentives for innovation and productivity."[29] "Here is an unresponsive monopoly, where innovation is seen as an insult to a 'a calcified system that sees change as a threat to its survival.' "[30]

School districts sometimes take on the unhealthy tendencies of any political institution; that is, the squeaky wheel gets the oil. It is true that schools tend to respond to public pressure, particularly if that pressure comes in the form of fifty parents from an affluent area marching into the superintendent's office. Poor and less educated parents do not always know how to apply the pressure. What results is a system that is inequitable on its face. However, different measures of accountability make it possible to make up for deficiencies in other parts of the city where parents are not equally mobilized. In the District of Columbia, the area west of Rock Creek Park is considered one of the city's most affluent neighborhoods. For years, it was commonly known that the neighborhood's schools—particularly its elementary schools—received more resources than schools in other parts of the city. That was largely because many of the parents had the means to supplement the schools' budgets as well as to lobby on behalf of their children's schools.

There are countless examples of PTA fundraisers where these schools' parents have raised additional funds to help pay a teacher's salary that otherwise would not be available, or to purchase supplies that otherwise would not be received. On many occasions, parents have helped pay for physical improvements that the school system could not afford. In turn, more affluent parents do not hesitate to remind the school system that they are footing the bill for many of their schools' resources. These circumstances permitted more active and conscientious parents to exercise a tremendous amount of power when they lobbied the school board, city council and mayor's offices for those resources directly within the city's control. That includes ensuring, among other things, that the city provided bus transportation for various field trips that were funded in part by parents, or demanding that the school system provide school personnel to help supervise activities sponsored by parents.

Also telling are those instances where parents from poorer neighborhoods have made a particular request from the school board for a long period of time. Often, it is only when the affluent parents or schools begin weighing in on the situation that the request is granted across the board. For example, for years there had been countless complaints in schools located in distressed neighborhoods about the quality of recreation facilities, athletic fields, and overall athletic programs. Those complaints continued for years. Over the past few years, the school system has begun responding. One of the main reasons was an aggressive lobbying campaign waged by parents from affluent schools to upgrade athletics.

In the District of Columbia, the Metropolitan Council of Labor includes all of the unions that have workers in the city. The teachers' union has emerged as one of the most influential members of that council. It is viewed as an activist union that has negotiated excellent contracts for its teachers. During the 1990s when the city was experiencing financial problems, teachers' salaries in the District did not keep pace with the national or regional average, but what the union lacked in raises, it made up for in various other perks, including a shorter workday and increased training and development.[31] But as strong as the teachers' union is in D.C., the city is not a "union town," in comparison to cities like Philadelphia, Detroit, and Chicago.[32] In D.C., while teachers' union leadership has developed close ties with elected officials and school administrators, the union cannot be directly blamed for the historical, bureaucratic failures of D.C. public schools. By and large, teachers' union leaders are primarily concerned about pay raises, benefits, and training for their membership. Occasionally, because of their close political relationships, the teachers' union leadership has attempted to flex its political muscle and engage in the traditional art of mutual back scratching. Many times they weigh in on selected aspects of the school system's bureaucracy. But again their impact is not as deep-rooted as in other cities.[33]

One contentious teachers' union issue is that of merit-based raises. In the District, there was a valid push for teacher pay increases since for many years our teachers were some of the region's lowest-paid. Working with the mayor and the school board, D.C. teachers received significant increases between 1999 and 2003. But even as teachers clamored about often well-deserved pay raises and benefits, they were undermined by their union representatives' objection to performance-based increases. Many teachers' unions, it seems, believe that pay hikes should occur as a matter of right and not in relation to a job well done. In any other industry, performance and evaluations are essential criteria in pay raise determinations. That apparent "innovation" has not caught on as quickly in education, which is probably one of the last areas where you can do a poor job and still get a raise. What does that say about our children's learning as a national objective?

Beginning in 2001, Mayor Williams and I hosted regularly scheduled meetings with then-Superintendent Vance, the school board president, the state education officer, and other school officials. In general, Dr. Vance was unflappable—the embodiment of the expression "never let them see you sweat." His demeanor has won him praise from many principals who feel that more than anything he brought stability to a system that was in complete disarray. At one particular meeting, Dr. Vance arrived, obviously agitated. He was clearly preoccupied and unfocused on the meeting agenda. I later asked Dr. Vance if everything was okay since it was so unusual to see him disconcerted. He explained that he was in the midst of negotiations with the teachers' union. Without going into great detail, he expressed how difficult it was for him to accept the idea that the teachers' union leadership was so dead set against having its member teachers work after hours—on their own time—in after-school programs, even if they wanted to! It was difficult to see how that was putting children first.[34]

One of the major problems with a top-heavy, politically driven teachers' union is the potential for corruption. I believe in unions and clearly see their utility in American life. However, there is no question that a corrupt union bureaucracy does an extreme disservice not only to its members but also to the public it is supposed to serve. There is no better example of this than the recent Washington teachers' union scandal. I received an urgent call one afternoon from a *Washington Post* reporter who asked if I had heard anything about misspending of teachers' union funds by Barbara Bullock, the union president, and Gwendolyn Hemphill, its treasurer.

There had been longstanding rumors and suspicions about Bullock and Hemphill blurring financial lines when it came to helping with Mayor Williams' controversial 2002 reelection, and so my initial hunch was that this latest story might in some way be tied to the election. (Gwendolyn Hemphill was also the chairman of the mayor's reelection committee. The mayor's reelection campaign had been a huge fiasco that ultimately led to national press coverage and a good deal of ridicule. Ultimately, the mayor was thrown off the ballot, but later won reelection with a well-orchestrated write-in campaign.)

Over the next several days and weeks, as the story unfolded, it became clear that the activities of Bullock and Hemphill amounted to the single biggest violation of public trust in the city's history. No official in any public role in local Washington, D.C. history had so violated his or her fiduciary duty, not even Mayor Boss Shepherd, who endured years of corruption allegations in the 1870s, or Marion Barry, whose drug conviction embarrassed the city.

It is estimated that Bullock and Hemphill misspent over $6 million in teachers' dues through an elaborate scheme that could occur based only on the unique relationship that teachers' unions have with financial offices in school districts. Based on union contracts and teachers' union dues obligations, a certain amount for dues is deducted from every teacher's paycheck. Those monies are deposited into the teachers' union account. Bullock and Hemphill were responsible for designating the amount to be deducted from teachers' paychecks. So instead of deducting, say, $1.80, they moved the decimal point so that $18 was removed. This practice took place over a six-year period, shortly after Bullock assumed the role of teachers' union president in 1996. The money was then appropriated by the two for personal use. Some of the expenditures were outlandish, including a million dollars on clothing, $20,000 worth of wigs, and many thousands more on furs, flat-screen TVs, and other luxury items.

As more and more information emerged about the extent of the allegations, all I could think of was Bullock's strident testimony before my committee on various issues that ostensibly reflected teachers' interests. I also find it fascinating that while frontline teachers are some of my strongest political supporters and I regularly receive complimentary notes and calls from teachers, my reception from the local teachers' union leadership has been cool at best, particularly since the emergence of charters.

For many of the same reasons relating to vested interests, I also have a fundamental disagreement with the notion of schools as moneymaking entities. Much like the current system where special interests cloud the real priority—education of children—I fear that interlacing education with profit-making goals can distort our compass. That is, if our schools are governed by market forces, education priorities may begin to take a back seat. This does not mean that for-profit entities should not be involved in education, but that education ought not be turned over wholesale to for-profit entities. At the end of the day, the primary responsibility for education lies with the state, and we have a fiduciary obligation to carry out that role.

Edison Schools, founded in 1992, is the country's largest private operator of public schools. As of 2003, Edison had implemented its school design in 150 traditional public and charter schools which enroll over 80,000 students.[35] It operates these schools under management contracts with local school districts and charter school boards. Like many other businesses across many sectors, over the past few years Edison has had financial problems. Its stock plunged 95 percent in 2002, forcing one state to advise its eighteen Edison schools to make contingency plans in case the company collapsed.[36] At the close of 2003, Edison appeared to be more financially stable.

Can we afford to entrust our schools to an entity that is governed by market forces? There is no doubt that when the company is doing well financially, school resources are plentiful. But what about those other times? There's a real question about whether the needs of constituent students will be negatively affected.

I'm also not completely sure that for-profit schools will ultimately work. If you're in the business of education, then you must at least allow your business motives to be deferential to the educational needs of the child. In a for-profit situation, that is somewhat counterintuitive. The business side of education must always make decisions that reflect the bottom line, and that may or may not be what's best for the child.

I have real concerns about turning over entire school systems to for-profit companies. It may make sense to do that with a handful of schools, but for dozens or hundreds of schools to be run by a business whose fortunes may depend on the state of the economy and whose demise may affect resource distribution for an entire school system, reliance on for-profit companies seems like folly.

Shortage of Quality Teachers and Principals

One of the most widely acknowledged problems of the public school system is the shortage of quality teachers and principals. There is no way to overestimate the influence of a good teacher on a young child. My first-grade teacher was a woman named Helen Shelton. She was the first adult other than my parents who expressed the utmost confidence in my potential to succeed. From the very first day I entered first grade she recognized that I was a little bit nervous, but also eager to learn. It may have helped that I entered first grade able to read because of my father's influence. Ms. Shelton constantly encouraged me, praised my work, and made me feel as though my future success in life was an inevitable reality. Largely for that reason to this day I remember her vividly, and she remains my favorite teacher!

Teacher effectiveness is the single most important factor driving student performance.[37] Studies show that, compared to inefffective teachers, top teachers can help enhance student performance by up to 50 percent. Faced with the prospect of filling more than two million teaching vacancies over the next decade, it is a travesty that recruiting, training, and retaining more high-quality teachers is not a top national priority.[38]

It is baffling that a 2003 report by The New Teacher Project[39] shows that the urban school bureaucracy's failure to act in a timely manner may also be sabotaging traditional schools' efforts to recruit good teachers, even as they hire unqualified teachers with friends in the system. According to this study of urban district hiring practices, because of aggressive recruitment efforts, high-quality teacher candidates regularly apply in large numbers to teach in large urban districts. However, they do not get hired because of the failure of the districts to make prompt job offers. Procrastination and hiring delays cause districts to lose substantial numbers of outstanding candidates to suburban school districts who typically hire earlier. The report's depressing findings showed that because of stepped-up recruitment efforts, high-quality teachers were applying in droves; that these stellar applicants often withdrew after months in limbo;

and that large urban districts were losing stronger applicants and hiring weaker ones.[40]

Until a few years ago, the D.C. school system had one of the oldest teaching corps in the country, which means that we had a fair number of teachers who had been in the system for over twenty years. Many of these are excellent teachers, but some are not as effective today because—simply put—times have changed. Children, technology, and ways of getting children interested in learning are different than they were even five or ten years ago. That's not to say that a good principal or teacher with twenty years' experience cannot be effective today. They must, however, be willing to upgrade and adjust their approach in order to connect with today's children.

In addition, even the best teachers are prone to experiencing burnout and/or becoming too immersed in the parts of their jobs that go beyond the school day, when they have to serve as brother/sister/parent/nurse/counselor to their young wards. Put mildly, teaching can be a grind.

In some cases, the requisite flexibility and willingness to embrace radically new technologies and methods has been beyond the ability or motivation of some veteran teachers. I recall one teacher who had won several Teacher of the Year awards. She had taught in a local high school in the city and had achieved near legendary status among former students. One evening, the local news showed her being led out of the school in handcuffs. She had gotten so frustrated with one of her students that she had repeatedly hit her. The extreme conduct was clearly out of character, but nearly everyone spoke of this teacher's frustration with "today's" kids. Sadly, many principals and teachers experience similar frustrations.

How can we best ensure that an otherwise stellar career of teaching our young is not marred by these kinds of tragedies? In addition to adequate teacher training and skills upgrading, it is also important to have a mixture of seasoned and new teachers in today's urban schools. The traditional school system has sought to bring in younger teachers and blend them into the school system. This approach does have promising and encouraging possibilities. In the District, organizations such as Teach for America have entered into a formal relationship with traditional public schools, as well as some charters, and have provided a number of competent and dedicated teachers to the system.

In the urban school districts, there is also a pressing need for more positive black male teachers and leaders. As I have moved in and around schools over the past several years, I have been struck by the fact that fewer and fewer men— particularly African American men—are in teaching and leadership positions in our schools. Many school administrators, in their quest for newer and younger teachers, have also been clamoring for more black males to teach in their schools. Schools also express the desire to develop mentoring programs with groups like Concerned Black Men, Big Brothers, and other groups where black men volunteer their time. This is significant because many of the children who are more prone to fall into juvenile delinquency or have lower test scores are African American boys. And many of these black boys come from single-parent, female-headed households. A 1991 study by the Bureau of Justice Statistics of the U.S. Department of Justice revealed that, nationwide, 53 percent of African American inmates incarcerated as a result of committing crimes come from households with no male figure.

Countless teachers, principals, and parents have expressed to me their experience that a positive black male teacher can have a tremendous impact on African American boys who otherwise will be lost to the streets. Recognizing that fact, many charter schools in the District have aggressively tried to recruit African American men to work in their schools. One such extraordinary young man is Brandon Lloyd, interviewed in chapter seven. Lloyd represents one of the best examples of charter school success with innovative teachers in the District. He is one of several strong black male figures in highly visible leadership capacities in their respective schools who have helped yield positive results within their communities.

Another critical and under-funded component to teacher recruitment and enhancement is teacher training and development. As bloated as most school districts and central administrations are, the one function that they must continue to maintain is teacher development. As with police and fire cadet programs, teacher training should include leadership development to prepare young teachers to assume more responsibility and eventually to become assistant principals and principals. In many instances, principals are appointed almost accidentally because they have been good teachers for so long that people turn to them naturally, even though they have not had the requisite training to understand and appreciate the complexities of being a principal. Today's principals, just like our teachers, often must undertake far more than their predecessors of twenty years ago, serving as social workers, politicians, business managers, facilitators, administrators, parents, educators, disciplinarians, and friends all in one. Many realize that they may be the only link some children have to a successful life. In the past that responsibility lay primarily with the parents, but now, in far too many neighborhoods it rests squarely on the shoulders of principals and teachers.

There is also near-universal consensus that a good principal can make a good school. Most jurisdictions struggle with the best approaches to develop, train, and nurture potential principals, recruit seasoned principals from other jurisdictions, and keep the good principals they already have. When I began to visit D.C. schools on a regular basis, I noticed that I could instantly discern the difference between various schools. One factor that made a significant difference was school leadership. You can feel it almost instantaneously when you're in a good school. Unfortunately, the reverse is also true, and that too often has a direct tie-in to poor leadership.

In the District of Columbia, members of the business community have worked with the mayor and the superintendent to begin an aggressive recruiting campaign to find and recruit the best principals around the country to lead some of our more troubled public schools. I am thrilled by this effort, but am also cautious about the way such recruitment is approached. In my view, it is critical for a principal coming in from outside the community to know and collaborate with local stakeholders and actors. Without understanding of and support from local elements, principals may be frustrated in their efforts to revamp a school and its leadership. That is why the more prudent approach would be not just to recruit new principals from around the country, but also to invest far more in training and development and, in instances where a new principal is brought in, to selectively place a seasoned assistant principal who knows the community in order to help provide stability for that school.[41]

The stifling aspect of bureaucracy for a principal is detrimental in two ways: Its rigid rules and regulations can strangle and frustrate principals, while other school leaders with potential see their development and growth limited by bureaucracy. They often fall into the habit of blaming the bureaucracy for things they cannot do, so much so that common mantras amongst principals and administrators include: "We cannot do it that way" or "We've never done it that way"—even about things they can do. Many new principals collide frequently with the bureaucratic limitations, but most eventually give up and begin to limit themselves, even where boundaries are not imposed on them. This is a phenomenon you will almost never see in a charter school. Charter school principals know from the beginning that they have free reign to recruit and hire the best possible teachers. They cannot fall back on the excuse that they can't do it this way.

Several years ago, various members of a PTA at a reasonably good school with active parents lobbied the school's principal about addressing the issue of a teacher who had received universal low marks from all parents. The principal acknowledged that the teacher was a problem, and said that she had petitioned central administration for another teacher. Thinking quite logically, the parents asked if they could advertise in order to try to recruit the best possible teacher. The principal rejected the idea, indicating that it was against the rules and that the superintendent would not allow it. She insisted that she could hire teachers only from an available list. The parents argued that this was not true. Facing resistance from the parents, the principal relented, agreeing to discuss the matter with the superintendent and head of the school board. The superintendent stated that while they generally encourage principals to choose teachers from a particular list, there was no rule to prevent an enterprising principal from finding and recruiting a teacher in some other way. With that concurrence, the parents ran an advertisement for available teachers. They received responses from as far away as Boston and Philadelphia. Several teachers from up and down the East Coast were clamoring to get into this school. After the process had ended and the teacher had been hired, the principal conceded that their final choice was far superior to any of the teachers on the approved list.

School districts throughout the country have crafted a variety of incentives to attract potential teachers and principals, including reduced rent in school-owned buildings, restaurant discounts, and gym memberships. But experts assert that discounts may not be enough. State and federal tax credits and/or subsidized housing benefits for teachers and principals would make a compelling official statement by the government.

Social Promotions

When I first became chairman of the education committee, then-superintendent Julius Becton had raised the issue of social promotions, and when Arlene Ackerman took over as his deputy, it was made clear that social promotions would be eliminated as a policy. Later, when the control board took over, social promotions were officially declared to be inconsistent with the District's education objectives. Prior to that time, children had been socially promoted as a matter of practice. I agreed with that declaration, but had major questions about what was being done to improve instruction and ensure that every child was getting what he or she needed in order to move legitimately from grade to grade. Even now, when social promotions are said to be explicitly against school district policy, I believe there are students being promoted who are not ready to progress, and that this takes place on a regular basis.

At one particularly poignant education committee hearing, a star female basketball player from a local high school delivered heart-wrenching testimony about her personal academic challenges with the D.C. school system. In front of several television cameras and a packed city council chamber, she recounted her learning experience starting in first grade when she was diagnosed as having a learning disability. She described her frustration when year after year, teachers and counselors who were supposed to help her advance academically failed to do so. As she entered high school and her basketball prowess emerged, she was still unable to read. But that didn't seem to matter. She was continuously promoted from grade to grade despite her clear lack of literacy. This young woman's story is not an anomaly. As of 2003, a student entering D.C. public schools has only a 50 percent chance of graduating. Many who do graduate cannot read at grade level. The District of Columbia adult literacy rate hovers at a tragic 37 percent.[42]

Lack of Parental Involvement

It is also wise to resist the urge to place wholesale blame on schools. Clearly, parents do have the primary responsibility to make sure their children get the educational opportunities they deserve. And yet too many children do not have nurturing parents who help steer them in the right direction. However, what if the parents are unable or unwilling to help? Shouldn't our public education system do all it can to fill in the gaps? It is clear that teachers and principals cannot replace parents, but the sad fact is that many teachers, particularly in lower income urban and rural settings are already doing just that. Nearly every teacher I know pays out of pocket on a regular basis to supplement the support and instruction that they provide to the children in their classrooms.

In an ideal world, parents are supposed to be responsible for raising their children, and good teachers and principals should be responsible for providing the education for these children. But more and more, we are seeing the result of two or three generations of children who grew up in households where they did not receive the nurturing, love, and attention needed to become productive adults. As a result, many parents never adequately learn how to be parents because they themselves never experienced good examples.

The question society must face in the wake of this reality is: How should our education system respond? The theory behind public education is that its doors are open to every child. Recognizing that not every child may have the same level of support at home, doesn't it make sense for the school system to be malleable enough to help compensate for the deficiencies in children's lives?

In 2003, my community was overwhelmed by an escalation of juvenile crime involving large numbers of automobile thefts. Large groups of teenage boys and girls were organizing, recruiting, and training fellow juveniles in the art of stealing cars, stripping them, and selling their parts. These children were so sophisticated that they were picking up and training new recruits even as some of their original leaders were arrested and placed in juvenile detention. One thirteen-year-old group leader had over ten arrests for auto theft in a two-year period. Like many of the other young people involved in these activities, that young man was living with a grandmother who could not control him. The juvenile justice system was not equipped to respond to such habitual juvenile offenders. These auto thefts crossed another dangerous threshold when the children started to race the stolen cars on city streets. In spring 2003, a fifteen-year-old boy was struck and killed by one of the stolen cars. A couple of months later, a long-time city worker was killed in a collision on her way to work after being struck by a stolen car being raced by another young teenager. For me, one of the most troubling aspects of this auto theft phenomenon was that the police were stopping children as young as eight and nine who were on the streets after midnight, developing the skills necessary to be promoted to leadership positions in these juvenile auto theft rings.

How should the government respond to situations like this? How can we force parents and guardians to be more responsible? And what should be the immediate community response? Working with several retired police officials who lived in my ward, I recruited a group of men who could provide individual mentoring for these youngsters. We made sure that each potential mentor received intensive training and made more than a superficial commitment to hands-on work with the children.

But this was not enough for many of the seniors in my community who were clamoring for tougher juvenile laws and who wanted to hold parents personally responsible for their children's actions. Following consultations with various community officials, social workers, and prosecutors, as well as reviewing best practices in other states, I introduced legislation in fall 2003 that established a means for legal accountability for irresponsible parents of wayward children. Under my proposed law, the parent of a juvenile with more than one arrest must attend a parenting class. After the second arrest, the parent faces forfeiture of public benefits, including welfare. Subsequent arrests bring harsher measures, including suspension of the parent's driving privileges. Along with these measures, the District of Columbia will make a stronger commitment to residential facilities where children can be placed when it is clear that they are receiving no guidance or discipline at home.

Of course, these measures do not provide direct solutions to the problems we see in many families. Nor do they adequately address the challenge educational systems have in attempting to solve social problems. But by placing more emphasis on parental responsibility, the educational and social needs of neglected children can be addressed before these kids are lost to the streets.

The Failure of Special Education

One of the biggest crises facing the public school system in the District today involves special education. The special education problem is a separate minefield in and of itself— often declared the number one problem by city leadership. For many years, our traditional school system has failed to deliver adequate special education services. We have not done a good job of assessing District children's special needs and providing the educational alternatives necessary to help them. As a result, the city has been under a form of court receivership whereby enterprising parents with lawyers can find alternative placements for their children and require the city to pay for them. We have special needs children being educated in places as far away as California and Utah, with the city paying for tuition costs as well as transportation costs for both children and families.

In addition, the school system mislabels some children as having "special needs" who may have behavioral problems that were not handled at an earlier age. Instead of full-time special education, these children require remedial help or psychological counseling. What results is countless young adolescents, particularly black boys, who may be misplaced in special education programs.

Due to the extraordinarily high costs associated with these failures, many of us in the District have been pushing for the city and schools to build in-house capacity to meet the educational needs of our children so they don't have to be shipped out of state. We also believe that many of these special-needs children can benefit from being included in the regular school atmosphere.

During 1999–2000, my committee spent several months investigating the problems of special education service delivery in the District. We saw countless experts and witnesses from around the country, who testified about best practices. We also heard from administrators, parents, and citizens. Finally, we held small group meetings with parents and teachers. At one of these meetings a young special education teacher who happened to be in her mid-twenties spoke candidly about the best way to solve the special education dilemma.[43]

She pointed out that one of the city leadership's main problems in special education was its failure to identify the disconnect between the school system's special-education services administration and its deputy superintendent for academic affairs. Practically, this teacher had a hard time getting support because as a special education teacher she was required to report directly to the special education division for all her needs, even as all the other teachers and principals reported to the deputy superintendent for academic affairs. The existence of two distinct hierarchies exacerbated the problem. When special education teachers asked one department for facilities, supplies, and resources, they were often told that they had to get them from the other department. This became such a problem that many special education teachers at the local level were relegated to closets and basement classrooms.

The teacher suggested that the only way to build in-house capacity in local schools is to ensure that any reform recommendations from the special services division are followed through by the deputy superintendent for academic affairs so that all classrooms—special needs or otherwise—go through the same channels. The teacher pointed out that all discussions about special education reform include only the special education teachers, but "here we are working with regular teachers and principals, who are not even at the table!"

What is the answer to our schools' special education problems? Of course, the inclusion model of incorporating special education children into mainstream classrooms where appropriate makes sense. Early assessments and quality implementation of each student's individualized education plan (IEP) is also important. Additionally, however, we need to upgrade our regular-education classrooms. Too many children get steered into special education because our traditional school system failed them in their early years.

More than anything, however, we need to change the tendency to treat children with special needs as second-class students. This negative culture continues to be perpetuated in most large school bureaucracies. It will only change when school districts place greater emphasis on the individual child's needs as opposed to preserving the "systems" designed to help the child.

Testing and Assessment

Requirements for testing and assessment have long dogged schools nationwide. Nowhere is that more evident than in my ward where teachers and principals are admittedly under the gun because of the annual Stanford-9 testing requirements. These professionals have now begun wholesale efforts to "cram" information into their students for several weeks prior to the test. All the while, a teacher may still have to deal with harsh daily realities such as physical abuse, drug use, and poverty.

For children suffering from extreme external forces, the

Stanford-9 test is not exactly a priority. Those circumstances must be addressed first before the child can be expected to learn and to perform on a test. Unfortunately our traditional system, unless pushed, does not account for those realities that confront our students and teachers every day. A child cannot learn at a basic level if she is inadequately nourished, lacks enough sleep because of problems at home, or has developed behavioral issues because of the environment she faces after the school day.[44] There is no doubt that testing is a critical means of assessing and maintaining standards, but testing must be conducted in the context of the individual needs of every child in a given classroom. Any authentic measurement must take place in the context of the realities in a child's life. While an independent determinant of a child's aptitude in terms of core subjects is critical, it is impossible to measure such aptitude when it is tested under hostile circumstances.

Educators must move with some dispatch to address those needs so that the learning environment is more productive and children are in a better position to learn what he or they need to for the standardized tests. Countless teachers have talked to me about children who fall asleep in class because of their parent's activities at night, or children who come to school hungry. These issues must all be scrutinized closely because they have a dramatic impact on children's ability to receive information, synthesize, and learn.

Many teachers struggle to fathom the true motivations behind standardized testing. These assessments force teachers, who know they will be judged on their students' performance, to concentrate their efforts on information they know is likely to appear on the test. The stakes are high. Teachers may lose their teaching contracts if their students perform poorly. Thus, consciously or otherwise, teachers pass the pressure on to their students by teaching to the test. Teachers object that, in the absence of this undue stress and provided with a meaningful learning experience, children naturally do well on these types of standardized tests. Of course, neither position is wholly without merit. Limiting instruction to test information makes little sense. At the same time, standardized tests can serve as critical indicators of success or failure.[45]

Of course, assessments now also have particularly dire consequences in light of the federal mandate, No Child Left Behind (NCLB), which was signed into law on January 8, 2002. NCLB represents the most sweeping reform of the Elementary and Secondary Education Act since it was enacted in 1965. It redefines the federal role in K–12 education to help improve the academic achievement of all students by increasing federal funding and oversight in state education policy. There are four basic principles in NCLB:

- Increased assessment and accountability, where each state and the District of Columbia is required to demonstrate that it has developed challenging standards for students in reading, math, and science; schools must show adequate annual progress, and must issue annual report cards on school performance and state-wide test results; after five years schools that fail to show adequate annual progress must be restructured by, for example, reopening the school as a charter, replacing curriculum and school staff, or turning the school over to the state or a private company.
- Greater emphasis on teacher quality standards, where public schools in which scores fail to improve over six years must change staff; all core academic classes (such as math and English) must be taught by qualified teachers by the 2005–2006 school year. "Qualified" is defined as at least a bachelor's degree, state certification, and demonstrated subject-area competency.
- Expanded education options for parents, where school districts are required to permit and assist students at struggling schools to transfer to a better school (including a charter) within the district; or students may receive supplemental educational services (such as tu-

toring, after-school programs, or summer school) funded by their schools.

• Expanded flexibility and local control in the use of federal dollars, where for the first time, most local school districts have latitude in determining how to use up to 50 percent of the federal funds they receive; rural schools and districts can determine how to spend federal funds on local priorities; and districts can explore ways of improving teacher quality.[46]

In 2002, I attended an awards banquet in my ward where outstanding public school principals, teachers, and students are acknowledged each year. Roughly six hundred people attend this banquet each year. The speaker was an undersecretary at the Department of Education who spoke about No Child Left Behind, and opined that Bush should be commended for being the first president in history to adopt such a policy. While this undersecretary was well meaning and distinguished—he had been a dean at several historically black colleges and clearly could relate to an urban setting—his attempts to champion the president in front of that particular crowd fell on deaf ears. The audience was polite but stoic.

NCLB has many progressive and interesting components and does indeed appear to go much farther than most of its predecessors. But a year later, is this new law affecting the change required to transform our public schools? A few years ago, Jesse Jackson, Jr. made a very interesting observation that has always stuck with me. He said that legislators always speak about their priorities so vehemently. They jump up and down, whoop and holler, and tell you that they support something. But at the end of the day, the only one that matters is the one who puts his money where his mouth is. All the others were just playacting. *You really want to know what someone's supporting? Follow the money!*[47]

A year in, it appears that No Child Left Behind is not matching its rhetorical support for education with the requisite financial backing.[48] The President has allocated about $7 billion more for elementary and secondary schools. However, the law adds many extra demands that cost money at a time when states are in the middle of budget crunches.[49] In the District, NCLB is revenue-negative. That is, it will cost more to implement than the grant revenues it earns. NCLB is expected to bring in approximately 530 dollars per child per year to the District's public (including charter) and private schools. However, NCLB mandates will cost 575 dollars per student per year.[50] Thus NCLB will cost approximately 45 dollars more per child than the District has dollars for.[51]

By 2005, DCPS is required to produce performance standards, develop an assessment system aligned with those standards, and create new assessments for English language learners, among other measures. This and other remediation necessary to bring school districts to basic levels of proficiency required under the Act will cost states millions. And that's money that the states largely have to come up with by themselves.[52] Add that to already thinning state education budgets due to declining economic conditions and school budget crunches throughout the country, and we are quickly heading for a real crisis.[53]

Leaving no child behind is a good thing, but it is also clear that the Bush administration is unequivocally committed to tying federal resources to test scores. At this point, NCLB has labeled thousands of schools across the country as failing schools.[54] Thus under NCLB, students in these schools have the option of transferring to a better school in the district. In 2003 in the city of Chicago alone, more than 19,000 students decided to exercise their options and ask for a transfer. The school system had only about 1,000 spots for them.[55] Are you doing the math with me? There is an interesting level of delusion operating here.

Tests should serve our children and schools, not the other way around.[56] Federal dollars should be used to help bring our children to the level where they can perform well on these tests. As it stands now, the government's policy resembles a 100-yard dash where a group of runners are required to start 50 yards behind the starting line, but expected to be competitive nonetheless. It's neither fair nor possible!

Some school districts have shown themselves unable to handle the job of bringing deficient schools up to speed in the proposed timeframe. In many communities, the need for remediation is total, complete, and across the board. So the logical end result of the government's policy could be urban communities with recognized blight being shut off from federal funds. These are the very communities and those are the very children we do not want to leave behind.

The key questions are, what do you mean by that remediation period? What type of remediation help are you going to provide? And who will manage that remediation? It is critical that we recognize when we are only pouring more money into a defunct system. For the federal government to make a real commitment to education, it will have to be very involved and must contribute to states' remediation efforts. Under the Act's different reporting requirements, states had to present their first NCLB plan in December 2002, at which time I held our first hearings on the Act in the city. The second plan was to be submitted in May 2003. As I have listened to witnesses at my education committee hearings and have spoken to educators in the District and throughout the country, I sense that there is a real level of skepticism about NCLB. School districts around the country are now a year into trying to put together an implementation plan.

Clearly there are some positive aspects to the plan. No Child Left Behind finally forces school districts in every state to honestly examine the way they educate children. Also, this is the first real attempt to put in place universal accountability standards that will ensure that school districts around the country are doing all they can to provide quality education to every child. There's utility to the Act's adequate yearly progress benchmarks (AYP) that call for schools to have a 100 percent proficiency within twelve years. One downside of the AYP is its correlation to standardized tests. In many school districts including the District, there is an inordinate amount of emphasis placed on these tests, causing many schools to teach the test as opposed to teaching kids the skills they will need to learn and continue learning. The challenge is being able to measure what works and what does not work in terms of teaching approaches. An equal challenge lies in the fact that we really can't take the same approach with every child because of the various socioeconomic factors that different children face.

NCLB also requires that school districts put in place alternative choice options for children who attend low-performing schools, and by that they mean charter schools. Each school district identifies the schools where there are problems and gives parents options to deal with the problems. In doing so, they may be able to save those children from potential failure. In response to the NCLB choice requirements, D.C. public schools identified fifteen under-performing schools and offered those children's parents the option to place their children in a new charter school. As in many districts, the number of seats available in higher-performing schools was limited and many parents did not take up the offer to transfer to charter schools. Only 209 parents actually sought transfers in 2002. (All children attending the fifteen under-performing schools had the option to transfer.) The reason for this seems to be the lack of education among parents who come from a lower socioeconomic status. They do not always know and appreciate what is right for their kids, and many may be fearful of change. Many families have ties to traditional schools that either they or their families attended, even if the school is not currently functioning properly.

NCLB ultimately is a way for the federal government to tie its offer of federal dollars to some increased accountability. The best way for states to act is found in the District's response to NCLB mandates: We would like to increase accountability; we want greater emphasis on teacher quality;

we want kids to do better on tests; we want expanded educational options for parents; and we want school districts to have expanded flexibility and local control in the use of federal dollars.

NCLB lays out the mandates and provides goals and timetables. All of that is good. School districts have a certain amount of time to implement NCLB requirements (for example, school districts have twelve years to comply with testing mandates). The potential failure comes in when school districts are slow to put in place the approaches necessary to meet these mandates. The solution lies in school districts using this mandate as an opportunity to think out of the box and put together their accountability plan so that it reflects the needs of children in their school districts. The accountability plan must move the local school district toward NCLB compliance.

In the District, DCPS submitted an accountability plan in December 2002 that theoretically addressed the twenty-seven NCLB criteria. That initial plan, which was the first submission, ultimately resulted in the District being viewed and judged as not having met any of those twenty-seven criteria. That, unfortunately, was not unusual. School districts around the country are just beginning to understand the serious import associated with NCLB and are realizing that the usual bureaucratic approach to filling out compliance plans and accountability plans are not going to cut it. School districts, including the District's, are going to have to be fundamentally honest about their shortcomings and committed to system change, or they will never meet the guidelines.

A good example in D.C. is the plan submitted in May 2003. One of the NCLB criteria dictates attendance monitoring whereby school districts track schools' average daily attendance. I was just amazed when I looked at DCPS's accountability plan: it showed an average daily attendance of 95 percent. This submission was so ridiculous on its face that it was almost laughable. Anyone who knows anything about urban school districts, particularly the District's, knows that schools are lucky to get 60 percent attendance because of the high truancy levels in neglected areas. Obviously the school district was lying.

As I looked at some of the individual schools where I knew there were high truancy rates and when I talked privately to some of the administrators, even they snickered. The school district claimed that it had reviewed the average daily attendance and done a random sampling. In reality they were not counting the kids who did not show up. That's just an example of how school districts cannot play with NCLB. They cannot get away with cursory and superficial reporting. They also cannot create a plan based on their reliance on faulty data.

I have introduced legislation in the District following a model in a handful of jurisdictions to ensure that school districts appreciate the seriousness of NCLB and the fact that it represents a new world order in educational outputs. I have taken DCPS's accountability plan that lays out goals and timetables in terms of how they will comply with federal requirements and added companion local legislation that in effect is a miniaturized version of the NCLB. In the local legislation, we have put in place our own local goals, timetables, benchmarks, and accountability standards that reflect what the school system says it's able to do, but that also reflects what is required in the federal law in a realistic way. For instance if one of the criteria is average daily attendance, our local law will put in place a reporting requirement that mandates an auditing process so that the reported attendance numbers are accurate and not just made up. We are reviewing every aspect of the NCLB law and comparing that with the DCPS accountability plan. We're extracting from the federal mandates local requirements to monitor implementation.

Every jurisdiction probably needs to follow suit with local legislation because it is unrealistic to rely on local school districts to instantly become accountable when the sheer nature of their bureaucracy flies in the face of accountability.

What happens when these timetables start to hit the
school districts? If school districts do not have 100 percent
proficiency within twelve years; if by 2007 states do not have
standards-aligned tests in reading, mathematics and science;
if they're unable to show adequate yearly progress; if test
scores do not increase—then these school districts will start
to lose federal funds. The real question is: What will happen
when that takes place and what will school districts and states
do in response? Recognizing that reality is upon us. As a
legislator, I feel that local lawmakers should provide the
practical and legislative push to their local school districts
that the federal government cannot provide because it is not
involved in the school district's daily actions. Local legislators must be engaged in providing legislative oversight to
ensure compliance.

The NCLB deadlines will hit over the next several years.
The law offers a great opportunity for expanding school
choice. From a local lawmaker's perspective, this is an opportunity to promote more charter schools, which are viewed as
part of the solution in NCLB.

CHAPTER 5

The Politics of Education

"Education is the most powerful weapon which you can use to change the world."

—Nelson Mandela

While an entrenched central bureaucracy is probably the biggest barrier to substantive school reform, another major obstacle is the "politics of education." Over the years, I've come to realize how easy it is to over-politicize various education reform initiatives. There is a tendency among elected officials to list education as the number one priority on their campaign's to-do list and yet to put education at the bottom of the list once they are elected.

State by state, city by city, among state legislators and city and county councilmembers, just a handful of elected officials are fully immersed in education-related concerns. Part of the reason for this has to do with the fact that education policy and legislative reform initiatives can be highly complex and politically sensitive. These initiatives often come with a tremendous political downside because of the traditional failures of most school bureaucracies. That is, it is hard to campaign on meaningful change in the school system when you are not in the best position to guarantee that change will occur.

This conundrum is further complicated by the practical reality of the school reform movement. Much of the discussion regarding changing the school bureaucracy seems to focus on traditional union-related issues and preserving the status quo. Most school bureaucracies are so adept at categorizing those who speak against them as being either anti-union or anti-kids that young, well-meaning legislators are often fearful of proposing anything that is really "out of the box" as it relates to education policy. The school choice movement itself reflects this tension.

As most opinion polls demonstrate, working-class African Americans are overwhelmingly in favor of school choice. Yet Democratic Party leaders have often fought against school choice because of teachers' union resistance. Democratic Party loyalists often counter cries for more school choice with calls for more funds. In other words, if you give the traditional schools enough money, they will effectively teach our children. As a newly appointed D.C. Council Education Committee chairman, I believed in that approach. My thinking was that if we could just get our public school system the money it needed, our problems would be solved.

It did not take me long to realize the fallacy of this position. If the system itself is fundamentally flawed and ill equipped with the approaches necessary to educate all children on their terms, then it doesn't matter how much money you allocate to that system.

I came to this conclusion after forcing myself to view the problems in our schools from a completely objective and nonpartisan perspective. As a traditional urban Democrat, that was not easy for me to do, considering the partisan pressures that can be brought to bear.

In 1997, when charter school legislation was passed in the District, the teachers' union took the public position that it would support charters, but wanted to ensure that teachers in the traditional school system did not start receiving less than their "fair share." Privately, it was clear among the union leadership that they did not welcome the coming of charter schools. The leadership found an ally in then-Superintendent Arlene Ackerman, who went on to engage in conflicts on issues where charters and traditional schools had points of disagreement.[57] Once I became a local advocate for charters in the school choice movement, I immediately drew the ire of our local teachers' union, so much so that when I ran for mayor in 1998, it ran TV ads with an X across my face, saying I was against teachers. Picture me explaining to my then-eight-year-old son that I really did like his and all teachers. All of that criticism was based solely on my support for charters. Those who go further in their support of school choice and embrace vouchers practically ensure ostracism by traditional Democrats and virtual castigation from the party.

I can speak to this type of political reprimand personally after supporting, along with the mayor and the school board president, a three-sector initiative whereby congress would fund public and charter schools, as well as vouchers. The three-sector funding strategy came on the heels of a proposal by President George W. Bush to offer additional federal dollars for the District of Columbia for a voucher program. Mayor Williams and I agreed to support that proposal provided that it would also include additional federal dollars for both D.C. public schools and charter schools. From my perspective, if we funded all three sectors and gave more funding to D.C. public schools, where most of the kids will always remain, we would only put ourselves in a better position.

Several weeks after this three-sector initiative was proposed, School Board President Peggy Cafritz wrote an editorial in support of vouchers. As one might expect, our traditional Democratic brethren roundly criticized the three of us, most notably Congresswoman Eleanor Holmes Norton, who continues to assert that vouchers are part of a Republican agenda designed to destroy public education. During the heated Senate debate over whether Congress would fund this three-sector initiative, senators on both sides of the aisle were weighing in. The actions of some reeked of partisanship. Some of the traditional arguments were that if Congress really wanted to help, they should give more

money to DCPS. Others felt that Congress should stay out
of the District's business. On the other side of the debate,
Republicans referred to the failures of DCPS and how D.C.
should be ashamed of itself for the way it was treating its
children.[58]

At one point, Eleanor Holmes Norton literally grabbed
hold of California Senator Diane Feinstein's arm and, wav-
ing her finger in the Senator's face, told her that there is no
way any true Democrat could support vouchers. After Congresswoman Norton finished her tirade, I walked up to Senator Feinstein. After laying out for her why I believed the
three-sector approach would ultimately help the city's children and serve to jumpstart reform, I urged the Senator to
take the approach that I believe needs to be taken on all
education-related issues: "If there is one issue that this country should approach on a nonpartisan basis, it is education.
This is an opportunity for you to cast a vote based on what
you feel will ultimately serve the best interests of children in
this city." Three days later, the Senator wrote an editorial
endorsing vouchers for the first time.[59]

Like most Democrats, I had always been skeptical of
vouchers, and there is no doubt that charters are far more
palatable than vouchers for the majority of people. The dis-
tinguishing aspect of charter schools is that they are designed to be more holistic and to address the needs of more
children in an individualized manner. In addition, charter
schools are schools of choice that are public, non-sectarian,
and open to all students. Vouchers, on the other hand, are
cash certificates of public funds that parents can use to send
their children to private schools, including religious schools.
For this reason, objections to vouchers have been made on
the constitutional grounds of separation of church and
state.[60] Vouchers raise the ire of opponents for a variety of
other reasons as well. It has been said that vouchers use selective admission practices and are "creaming" the best and
brightest students from the public schools, that they do not
serve students with special needs, that they do not improve

students' academic achievements, and most hysterically, that thy are part of a scheme to destroy public education![61]

I still do not believe that vouchers are the "complete answer" to reforming public education. In reality, too much time and energy is spent on the issue of vouchers since under the best of circumstances only a handful of children benefit from them.[62] The proposal endorsed by the mayor and me was means tested, thus ensuring the participation of children from households below the poverty levels. We also insisted that accountability measures be put in place to quantitatively assess how the children were faring in the schools that received vouchers.

But traditional Democratic Party loyalists believe that vouchers are a first step in the ultimate destruction of public education. Their view is that diverting public dollars that could go to public schools and putting those dollars into private schools ultimately depletes and eventually destroys traditional public schools. This concern seems alarmist, since under the best circumstances in the District of Columbia, private schools can only absorb a small number of the city's school-age children. Under our three-sector proposal, just 2,000 children would be able to avail themselves of vouchers, while 11,000 would remain in charters, and 64,000 in public schools.

I have come to believe that there is an even stronger reason to support school choice in all forms. This has been evidenced by the success of charters in the District of Columbia. No matter what union officials or traditional-school activists say, it is abundantly clear that traditional school systems never have and never will reform themselves internally. Truly meaningful and sustainable school reform can occur only through external pressure, and the best form of external pressure is school choice. Therefore, if a school district has options for parents that take into account the disparate needs of children, public officials have an overriding obligation to fund those measures and maximize each child's potential output.

One of the most unfortunate realities of the school reform movement is the labeling and marginalizing that occur when something new and unique is proposed. I disagreed with former New York City mayor Rudy Giuliani on a whole host of issues, but he was once criticized for saying that traditional public education should be blown up. Like it or not, he may not have been too far off base. While most traditional school districts can be reclaimed, the best way to salvage them is by forcing them to mimic or mirror models of local school autonomy where parents feel empowered, teachers can teach, and principals can run their schools without overriding interference from central administrations. The sooner elected officials and policymakers recognize this, the sooner we will move toward true school reform.

I came to support vouchers and all aspects of school choice, including home schooling,[63] after viewing the problems of education from a totally objective and nonpartisan basis. It is my fervent wish that there will come a day in this country when decisions regarding education-related matters will be made without any deference to the party politic.

CHAPTER 6

Innovation by Charter

"We have a powerful potential in our youth, and we must have the courage to change old ideas and practices so that we may direct their power toward good ends."

—Dr. Mary McLeod Bethune

A growing body of international research has highlighted several factors associated with high educational quality and school effectiveness, including sufficiency of facilities and resources, parent and community involvement in education and schools, clear academic goals, high student expectations, employment of high-quality and motivated teachers, creative use of first-rate instructional materials, ongoing teacher training and professional development, and a supportive policy environment, among other factors.[64]

Many of these factors are encompassed in a uniquely domestic innovation—charter schools.[65]

Charter schools began as a pet project of free-market disciples. The movement had its origins in a number of other reform ideas: alternative schools, site-based management, magnet schools, public school choice, privatization, and community-parental empowerment. In the 1970s, New England educators proposed that small groups of teachers be given "charters" by their local school boards to explore new approaches in education. Later, in the 1980s, Philadelphia established its own form of "charters," a number of experimental schools-within-schools, some of which were schools of choice. This idea was further developed in Minnesota where schools were formed according to three basic values: opportunity, choice, and responsibility for results.[66] The reasoning was that if parents who could not afford private tuition had alternatives to the failing public schools, they would seek out and choose those alternatives. And indeed they have. In 1991, Minnesota passed the first charter school law, and the first charter school opened its doors in 1992. Since then, school choice has quickly expanded to become a popular movement and charters have flourished at a phenomenal rate: As of 2003, about 685,000 students were attending 2,700 charters in thirty-seven states (and the District of Columbia).[67]

D.C. has one of the country's most successful public charter school clusters. As of 2003, there were almost forty charter schools educating roughly eleven thousand children—17 percent of all public school students in the District. This represents the nation's highest percentage of children in charter schools and an extraordinary number considering that the first charter school opened its doors in the District only six years ago. The irony of charter schools' popularity in the District is that in this heavily Democratic, mostly black and low-income city, parents who often know nothing of the origins of the conservative movement instigated by school choice ideologues—many of them veterans of the Reagan-era education department—have embraced the schools with open arms and as an alternative to a system that chronically fails their children.[68]

In the traditional sense, charters are public schools. They are supported in large part by public funding. They are open to all students. And although free from many of the bureaucratic shackles that constrict their traditional counterparts, charter schools are also overseen by public agencies, which hold them responsible for the academic and fiscal goals laid out in their charters. Of course, charters are also ultimately beholden to the public, who may choose them or not.[69]

Depending on its laws, each state differs on which body

may approve charters, who can operate a school, what the teacher certification requirements are, and how independently a school may operate.[70] Charters are bound by health and safety regulations, and any school that receives federal funds must observe federal mandates for the use of those funds. In general, charter applicants must submit business plans outlining the proposed school's mission, its governance and management structure, its academic design (curriculum, subjects, performance standards, instruction methods), its assessment techniques, and other issues such as professional development, partnerships, parental involvement, and community outreach.[71]

The beauty of a charter school is that it allows for creativity and autonomy to exist based on the vision of a handful of community members. For this reason, charters tend to have widely diverse missions and approaches to education, and to some extent, these varying approaches have led to their success.[72] At the same time, it is my experience that some of the most successful charter schools have striking commonalities in their underlying principles that seem to contribute to their overall success. These are qualities that successful traditional public schools also share in, but because of the bureaucratic and other constraints discussed above, traditional schools are hard-pressed to establish these needed reforms.

Most charter schools are much smaller than traditional public schools.[73] Their academic standards and approaches to learning are much more diverse and innovative. Decentralization and the freedom from the many layers of bureaucracy in traditional public schools is a huge advantage for charters. In most charter schools, the buck stops with the principal or founders. Parents, teachers, and principals also seem to be more satisfied with charter schools. Principals have greater independence and latitude in school management, and teachers are given much greater flexibility to try more innovative instruction methods.[74] In the District of Columbia, large numbers of charter school founders, principals, and teachers hail from the DCPS. My extensive discussions with these former DCPS staff reveal that they are thrilled about their newfound freedom from bureaucracy, the smaller class sizes, and the buoyant academic environment.

Some charters focus on children with greater academic and social needs and thus have developed customized methods to address all such aspects of a child's needs. Community hub schools take this concept a step further by also addressing the needs of their students' families and immediate community. In many instances, charters have demonstrated far greater success than traditional public schools in re-engaging alienated students who have been marginalized by the traditional system due to their particular demands and need for focused attention. These students have had difficulty becoming engaged, challenged, and supported in mainstream schools, but seem to thrive in charter schools.[75]

While charters are required to participate in some nationwide assessments, in general they are held to a slightly different accountability measure than their public counterparts. In the District, a charter represents a contract between the grantor and the charter applicant/founder. The contract essentially outlines the conditions of the management, operation, and education program of the charter school. Thus, the school would be accountable for meeting the terms of its own charter rather than the rules and regulations of the local school district. A charter school can be closed by the sponsoring organization if it does not meet the terms and conditions outlined in its charter.[76]

Tensions have grown in tandem with charter school enrollments as the obvious financial implications for traditional public schools have hit home. In D.C., for example, when the city switched to a per-pupil funding formula, dollars allocated for public education were tied to the number of students in the system—that is, the money follows the children. Clearly, if charter schools continue to grow at the same extraordinary rate, then by definition less money will flow to traditional schools. This issue is a primary concern of charter school critics. In order for traditional schools to maintain their current funding levels, they have to find ways of retaining their current student population.

Interestingly, in various interviews D.C. Superintendent Vance noted that the movement has not been just one way—that is, out of the traditional public schools to the charters, but often children attending charters have switched back to traditional schools, sometimes in mid-year. While there are no hard numbers to confirm such a phenomenon, I personally find this type of movement healthy. This is the essence of competition: choice and options. Parents have a greater opportunity to seek out and choose the best school setting for their children, whatever that may be.[77]

One of the criticisms against charters involves their skimming the cream of the crop—that is, the best students—from public schools. In my experience in the District, this has been far from true. Large numbers of the District's charter school students come from low-income neighborhoods and communities of color.

A great deal of research is focused on the academic performance of charters relative to traditional schools, and both charter advocates and opponents can produce studies from credible sources supporting their particular positions. In general, it appears that in their first few years, most charters do not show major assessment differentials from their traditional counterparts. Charter advocates claim that initial assessment results for charter students are misleading because when students first transfer into a charter, they are often academically lagging, having been socially promoted from one year to another. It is only after students have had several years to experience the school's academic rigors (or lack thereof) can a student be accurately assessed and accurate comparisons between the two schools done.[78]

National studies also differ widely on whether charters' impact has been positive, negative, or neither. Charter advocates claim that the schools are central to the attempt to restore the nation's ailing education system and that they are accelerating system-wide improvements. Opponents scoff that that not only do charters have the same dysfunctions as traditional schools, they serve as a drain on resources that could otherwise be spent on improving the system. The most extreme see charters as a "far-right-wing attempt to destroy public education!" It is conceivable that the two school tracks—currently distinct—may eventually evolve into a unitary system where unique and distinctive schools are available to all parents. In addition, the proliferation of the charters may drive essential reforms such as perhaps eliminating some of the more troublesome characteristics of the traditional education bureaucracy. And at the very least, it seems "[e]ven in areas with no [charter schools], evidence of the impact of the [charter] initiative can be seen in the renewed debate over the quality and performance of public schools."[79]

Major findings of nationwide charter school surveys compiled by the Center for Education Reform from the 1997–98 and 1998–99 school years show the following:[80]

- Charter schools deliver the smaller size that parents want. Average enrollment is about 250.
- Two-thirds of charter schools have significant waiting lists.
- A majority of charter schools are approved by an agency other than the local school board. Local boards are more likely to grant charters where state law allows for multiple charter-granting bodies.
- Charter schools serve large percentages of children who are typically underserved in America's schools.
- Curriculum programs vary widely; the top five are all known for their academic rigor and integrity: science/math/tech, core knowledge, thematic instruction, back-to-basics, and college prep.
- Although two-thirds of schools responding were less than three years old, 39 percent reported only evi-

dence of academic improvement, including gains in reading and math performance, test scores that are higher than district and state averages, increased parental involvement, higher attendance, and fewer discipline problems.

Charter schools in the District initially met with a great deal of resistance from the education "establishment." I myself was initially skeptical about charter schools. At that time our schools were in shambles. The facilities were dilapidated, the roofs in disrepair, and the kids were not learning. Consequently, the public schools had been placed in receivership. From my point of view, representing a ward in Southeast D.C. where we have both some of the best and some of the most troubled aspects of the city, I was well aware of the disparities in the public school system and knew the challenges that had to be overcome. Some of the schools were simply not doing their jobs.

Against this backdrop, I had an ear open for something different, and that is what the charter school movement offered. My knowledge of charter schools at the time did not extend far beyond the national Edison schools. I saw these schools as another manifestation of folks outside the community imposing their will over local school districts. Of course, this perception was born out of ignorance. In time, I was able to meet with numerous advocates and education activists, and it really sank in that charter schools were an experiment that could work—not just as effective entities by themselves, but also as a means of jumpstarting reform in traditional public schools.

As I began to hold hearings on charter schools and to understand some of the unique offerings that were proposed, the schools became more attractive as an alternative. The diversity of the new crop of charter schools was fascinating. From adult education to special needs, charter schools were proving themselves to be relevant. For example, the hospitality charter school focused on children interested in

going into that industry, and it provided a clear tie-in between education and career. This sort of relevance was something we had long talked about in the context of the
traditional public schools.

In 1995, there were home-rule issues surrounding the
charter schools, which operated under two separate pieces
of legislation: federal and local. The D.C. Council had just
passed the charter school legislation, providing that the
school board could grant charters. The council felt strongly
that there were parallel interests at play: It was important for
the charter schools to be autonomous and equally critical
for them to live up to their charters. The D.C. City Council
charter school legislation literally proceeded simultaneously
with the federal legislation. As the council was drafting its
legislation, council members became convinced that the
best way to get buy-in from the board of education was to
give the board chartering authority. Otherwise, they reasoned, the board members were more likely to become ob-
stacles to the charter school.[81]

Following a disturbing 1996 report on D.C. public
schools, the federally appointed financial control board removed the superintendent, stripped away the elected school
board's authority, and took over D.C. public schools.[82] The
board of education retained one power: selection of charter
schools. At the same time, Congress had enacted charter
school laws and enabling legislation to maintain control over
the process. Under the federal statute, the Charter School
Board was charged with reviewing and approving charters.
This statute also gave charter schools more latitude, thereby
curtailing the ability to monitor and engage in oversight. In
1997–98, the first three charter schools opened in the District, approved by the Board of Education.

From the very beginning, there was tension between the
federal and local chartering authorities: the D.C. Public
Charter School Board and the board of education. Prospective charter applicants often agonized over which entity to
apply to for their charters: federal or local. For example,

when going through his determination process, Community Academy's Kent Amos chose to apply with the board of education because he wanted to support the body elected by the local community. He reasoned that it was important for the local school board to have a role in selecting strong, viable charter schools. Many others chose to apply with the federal board.[83]

The remaining lingering tension between the two boards is that the public charter school board is unquestionably committed to the viability and success of charter schools, while it is unclear whether everyone on the board of education has that same commitment. Most of the schools chartered by the board of education have worked because of two individuals with primary responsibility for directing the effort on behalf of the board: Shelby McCoy and Linda McKay.[84] These women have been committed to the board of education's chartering process and have done a good job of processing applications and ensuring that good schools receive charters. They have performed a delicate dance because certain board members are not charter supporters. To the staff's credit, applicants to the board of education find that their applications have been processed in competently. This has led to the board granting some good charters.

The two chartering bodies' attitudes on charters are based on political realities. While the public charter school board has always been committed to strong charter schools, the notion of charters was thrust upon the board of education by council legislation. It was a power that some board members grappled with because they were fundamentally against the notion of charters. So while the public charter school board was serving the role of advocate and authorizing agent, the board of education chartering representatives were clearly more muffled in their advocacy role. Some viewed their chartering responsibility almost as a chore rather than a passion.

The tension between these two bodies came to a head at oversight hearings on charter schools' progress. The board of education and charter school board were not particularly comfortable attending hearings and testifying together. I found this alarming, so I often required the two bodies to sit together and consult. As chairman of the board of education, I was able to demand that they coordinate efforts and periodically compare notes on the facilities issues. In the next oversight hearing, I would ask them how often they had met.

Board of education staff members, such as Shelby McCoy, itched to work more closely with the charter school board, but were frustrated by their superiors. At the hearings, board of education representatives attempted to do all the talking; however, after hearing opening statements, I would pose questions to the staff including the executive directors from the public charter school board and the board of education. My goal at those hearings was to place the charter schools' progress on the record, not in a superficial way, but on a hands-on day-to-day "this is what we are doing" level.

There appears to be more coordination now, in part because we are at the point where charter schools nearly have traction. Seventeen percent of all District students are attending charter schools, and that is indicative of some entrenchment. There are also a number of households where one child attends a charter school and the other a traditional public school. Because of the movement back and forth, and the fact that a large number of District children—roughly eleven thousand—are in charter schools, a certain level of collaboration has almost been forced on the system. There are unique issues in each of the charter schools that must be responded to, and they cannot be shielded by way of a central administration. For example, in order to immunize children, the health department has to interact with each individual charter to ensure that the school's children are properly inoculated. For the traditional public schools, all the health department has to do is go to the superintendent's office. For charters, each school is separate, with its own autonomous administration. This situation forces charters to address some issues in a collaborative way, regardless of which body issued their original charter!

In 2002, charter school leaders approached me about finding a way for federal funds for needy families (known as TANF) to be made available for all schools with after-school programs. Through a technicality—the law that provided the funds mentioned traditional public schools by name—charters were not permitted to share in those dollars. I put an amendment in the budget that would allow charter schools to share in the federal funds, thus allowing charters to have after-school programs similar to those of other public schools. In this instance, both the federally and locally chartered schools were lobbying me for the federal funds. At one point, they began collaborating and lobbying together. School representatives from both sides came to me jointly.

Increasingly, the entire charter school community has banded together on issues that are mutually important to them. Their interests are essentially the same, and it does not matter which authority granted them their charter. All are charter schools facing both subtle and overt hostility from the traditional school system.

Two years ago, I proposed legislation to merge the two tracks of charters. I believed at the time that I would have the support of the charter school community. To my profound surprise, my proposal was shot down resoundingly. I was amazed that the board of education, which had fought charter schools for so long, argued against merging the two boards and bragged about the great schools they had picked. I had envisioned disempowering the board of education and felt that too many obstructionist tactics were originating from that quarter, making it hard for even their own charter school administrators to do their jobs. My proposed legislation never even made it out of committee but, ironically, it did force the board of education to state publicly its profound support for charter schools! They were forced to act more like supporters because they realized that they enjoy the power of granting charters. I like to believe that the proposed legislation served a good purpose.

The District's charter schools have made some meaningful gains over the past several years.[85] For example, a majority of those schools chartered and monitored by the Public Charter School Board showed improvements in spring 2001 test results.[86] According to the board, ten of thirteen schools included in the report advanced in national rankings in reading, while ten of thirteen schools advanced in mathematics.[87]

In addition, the D.C. Public Charter School Board reported the following gains:[88]

- Nine of eleven grades showed an increase in the percentage of students at "Basic" or above in reading, while eight of eleven grades showed an increase in math scores.
- The percentage of students scoring above the national average on the NCE scale increased from 26 to 30 percent in reading, and from 29 to 33 percent in math.
- Eight of twelve schools increased NCE Mean Scores in both reading and math. Only one school decreased in both categories. In ten of twelve schools, the percentage of students scoring Basic or above in reading increased; in five schools, the percentage of students scoring Basic or above in math increased.
- There was a slight falloff in "gain scores" from the previous reporting year. The average student gained slightly less than a year in both reading and math, and the percentage showing more than a year of gain was slightly less than last year. About half of all students gained at least a full year in both reading and math.
- Gains were relatively stronger at the middle and secondary levels than at the elementary levels.

The Public Charter School Board specifically lauded three schools that had shown significant improvement:

- Cesar Chavez Public Charter High School for Public Policy posted solid gains in reading and outstanding gains in math. With "zero" meaning at least one full year of academic progress, the average student gained 4.9 NCEs in reading and 21.8 NCEs in math. The gains were broadly shared as well, with 62.5 percent of students gaining at least a full year in reading, and 92.5 percent showing at least a year's improvement in math.
- Meridian Public Charter School had solid average gains in reading (3.7 NCEs) and math (8.9 NCEs). Gains were distributed broadly, with 71 percent of students gaining at least one year in reading, and 83 percent gaining at least one year in math.
- SEED Public Charter School showed impressive gains (4.9 NCEs) in math, with 77 percent of the student body gaining at least one full year.[89]

CHAPTER 7

Six Exceptional D.C. Charter Schools

"Education is not the filling of a pail, but the lighting of a fire."

—William Butler Yeats

This chapter describes six exceptional charter schools in the District of Columbia. In examining these schools' experiences, five principle areas stand out as the foundation for their success. The schools profiled here have:

- A baseline expectation of excellence and high academic standards
- Comprehensive and pre-set missions that permeate all aspects and operations of the school
- Innovative approaches that fit the needs of individual students, recognizing that there is more than one way to engage and invigorate a child
- Close connections with the immediate and larger community as well as relationships with private-sector companies and social/political organizations
- A tendency to shy away from one-size-fits-all practices as they relate to many aspects of school life, including the hiring of teachers and guiding students[90]

Community Academy

The Community Academy is a bustling, colorful bazaar of students, teachers, administrators, and volunteers. With bright halls and classrooms, and fresh air wafting through the halls, the Academy looks and smells well funded. The atmosphere is festive, with sounds of play and learning bouncing from every corner. A wall in the main office boasts a large board featuring photographs of staff and teachers, along with narratives of their hopes and dreams for the upcoming school year and beyond. We learn later that there is a similar board with photographs and accompanying narratives in each classroom for every child, teacher, and administrator in the school. "We do it every year," notes Kent Amos, the Academy's founder, with a smile. Children come in and out of the front office to sharpen pencils and run other errands. They interact affectionately with the staff, a group of young black women who dispense encouraging words and pet names generously. These women evoke feelings of high praise: Firm! Competent! Serious! Loving! Americorps volunteers reading with the children pepper the halls.[91]

With 540 students enrolled, the Community Academy is virtually bursting at the seams and is in need of a new facility. The school administrators have tried—sometimes with great difficulty—to limit the classes to twenty students each. The Academy includes dedicated classrooms for special education and Spanish. It also has classes for adults and a computer lab, although there are also computers in every class. Students in the classrooms appear engaged, happy, and active.

Barbara Nophlin, until recently the Academy's director, explains that many of these classes were previously "from hell," and that some of them are now virtually unrecognizable. The Academy's students come from different schools for a variety of reasons. Many of the students here have "issues—one just got back from a lockup hospital, another

watched his mother die . . . it's brutal." For these and other
reasons, the Community Academy has specialized full-time
staff, including a psychologist, a social worker, and a special
education team.

Community Academy is a family-based, community-cen-
tered school with a whole-child approach to education. To
educate the child, the school embraces the entire community, especially parents, as partners. In pre-kindergarten
through seventh grade, students are challenged to excel and
to be involved in their communities. The youngest students,
those in pre-kindergarten through first grade, are assisted in
the classroom by student helpers. Students in grades four
through seven are taught by teams. In this family-based
learning environment, parents serve on the Board of Trustees and hold regular meetings. They are currently forming
a Parent Advisory Group. Some are leaders and meal coordi-
nators at Kid's House, an after-school program that offers
homework assistance as well as enrichment and recreational
opportunities. All parents are required to volunteer at the
school.

The community is also essential to the educational process. It is, in fact, the connecting piece in a seamless web of
care that the school seeks to provide for all of its students.
Community Academy is dedicated to the whole person, the
whole family, the whole community. It is a creative work-in-
progress.

Amos exudes the dynamic magnetism we have observed
in the leaders of many successful charter schools. He speaks
passionately about the Community Academy in the context
of a much bigger strategy. Years ago, Amos and his wife
started doing NGO work in their own home—something
they called the Urban Family Institute. They worked primarily with the neighborhood kids because they felt that everyone in the neighborhood had a part to play in the children's
development. "You need equal parts capacity and passion,"
Amos has always believed, "You evaluate what your expertise
is and you use your capacity where it's most important."

Amos and his wife felt that they had a lot of experience and training to offer.

The Urban Family Institute was a success, but many of the kids couldn't escape the realities of the neighborhoods they were living in. Over the course of a year, Amos buried six of the kids from the Institute. He was devastated, but his pain drove him to do something globally—in scale with the purpose of structural change—"something worthy of my kids' sacrifice."

How do you affix to a school other elements that go beyond the moment? That was the question Kent Amos sought to answer when he created Kid's House. Kid's House is an environment; it's the engagement of adults in the lives of the children in a community—primarily through volunteerism.

What do you have in every community that's public and nonsectarian? Schools! So Amos and his colleagues focused in on the schools as the center of the community. Unfortunately, they discovered that the bureaucracy of public schools was not amenable to the change they were trying to create. "We were not feeling supported in the way that was our due," he states matter-of-factly.

It so happened that the charter school movement presented itself at the most appropriate time. They started looking at the charter schools as a means of not only teaching their children, but also of developing the community. The outcome of their efforts, the Community Academy, is an institution that seeks to transform both child and adult. Amos and his colleagues worked with a number of professionals who put the school together and translated the dream into a conceptual framework. That framework, incidentally, is being used in after-school programs in seventeen states.

Kent Amos absolutely believes in the value of the existing school system. The only difference is that he believes in maximizing the existing capacity, rather than thwarting or frustrating it. Every one of the Community School's leaders has come out of the D.C. public schools. The Community Academy went out and hired D.C.'s principal of the year and the runner-up. The school even hired a pediatrician because it realized that the overall health of the community was poor.

Even now, Amos finds that the city's bureaucracy undermines his school's progress. For example, the Community Academy has an ongoing dilemma about its facilities. In the past, if a school building was available and a public school needed a facility, the city would give that facility to the school—that is, school property was always to be used for school purposes. That has not been the case with charters, even though charters are part of the public school system and serving the same children. Ideally charters and traditional schools would be sharing facilities and sharing programs, but the traditional public school system has not embraced the notion that both are part of one system.

Amos speaks of his desire to create the ideal conditions under which innovations being practiced in one school would flow into all public schools. He hopes to take the creativity to scale.

The Community Academy enjoys solid relationships with many public and private enterprises, including the police and the Metro trains and buses. The school partners with Learn Now for curriculum development and teacher training, and with Cisco for the purpose of improving system capacity. Other aspects of their program are funded by the Walton family and the Mott Foundation.

Friendship Edison School

Friendship Public Charter School is a multi-site charter school, with four school campuses that serve 2,907 children in grades K–12.[92] The Friendship school is the largest charter school in the country, located in northeast and southeast D.C., in renovated school buildings that had been closed and were deteriorating. The students are 99 percent African American and overwhelmingly from poor and working-class families. These children are thriving at Friendship schools.

Friendship House (FH) was an old-line social service

agency founded in 1904 as a settlement house. Set up originally as a community development corporation, Friendship House had job training, daycare, and senior citizen programs. But while it had always been effective as an organization, Friendship House was not focused on the future.

In 1996, Donald Hense, who had been on the FH board since 1973, was asked to take over the executive director role. He accepted, with the caveat that the board had to agree to change the organization's primary focus to addressing the problems of children. The FH leadership concurred, shifting the organizational focus to solving problems as early as possible rather than waiting until later. FH pulled together a task force led by D.C. public school teachers, administrators, and counselors. They met over a period of six months to discuss what could be done about the deteriorating state of public education in D.C.

When the board first sat down with the task force, it did not know anything about charter schools. At some point in the process, the board became apprised of the charter concept, and immediately began to discuss establishing a charter school. It was clear that a lot of charter organizers rallied behind the issue of public education, rather than around establishing a charter school for its own sake. They were all, in essence, public education advocates.

At a meeting at Vassar, Hense met Deborah McGriff, Director of Development for the Edison schools. He invited her to Washington to discuss charters and how FH could get one established. FH researched the Edison curriculum and design. Hense himself had always been a fan of project-based education and understood that while some children could learn by sitting in a seat and listening to a lecture, others learned better by working on a project.

McGriff came to town and brought the founder and CEO of Edison. Less than two hours later, the FH board was convinced that Edison as a corporation really had focused on children, and that it was serious about improving education. Nor did Edison appear to be shy about locating in urban areas where schools were difficult to manage. A partnership was close at hand.

FH forged ahead, applied for its charter, and started to look for real estate. Within the year, FH had opened two elementary schools. Edison's investment was critical because Friendship House was a small organization and would have been able only to start with grades K–3 and then add a grade each year. That scenario, they felt, was a potential disaster in terms of overcoming public skepticism about whether the charter would work.

FH knew it was on the right track. Edison came forward with plans for loaning FH money to invest in redeveloping buildings that had closed down and were dilapidated eyesores in good neighborhoods. (FH has since purchased three of its buildings.) FH established the board of its charter schools, including parent representatives, educators, and business people. It looked for people who knew the difference between being on a board and making policy. It established a board that does not "meddle" by going through the school building and interfering with education. Rather, these are board members who understand education and finance, and collectively provide a strong mechanism to support the schools.

Hense feels that Edison may not be for everyone and does not necessarily work everywhere. In some places where Edison has had free reign, its record has been shaky. But he has found that Edison works well where it works for someone—as it does in Washington, for Friendship House. Edison manages the FH schools and has a clear understanding under contract of what FH expects at the local level. FH also has provided Edison with a lot of room to interpret its design so that it meets the FH needs. On the other hand, Edison has clear-cut accountability standards and goals that it must meet; for example, Edison is required to report quarterly to Friendship House.

Donald Hense is unconcerned about Edison's failures in other cities; his only concern is what they are doing in D.C., and in D.C. Edison appears to be doing an extraordinary job.

Under the charter school model, the principal is the COO of the school so the principal controls the budget. Under the Edison model, there is no large central administration associated with the school. There are, for example, fewer than two hundred staff members running Edison's central office. Their profit is derived through economies of scale.

Like Kent Amos's Community Academy, FH believes in educating not just a child but an entire family and whole neighborhoods. According to Hense, "Parents can be a bigger problem than the children, particularly if they don't have a vision of future for themselves." To address the needs of both parents and children, FH has a community technology center in one of its schools that educates welfare mothers, teachers, and children from the projects. The schools also provide adult education.

The school itself is a unique academic institution with an academic program that sets high standards for every student. The curriculum and instructional methods draw from proven programs, such as the Success for All reading program developed at Johns Hopkins University and Everyday Mathematics developed at the University of Chicago. The school's teachers are trained to use assessment data to focus instruction where students most need help. The students benefit from a safe, vibrant, and disciplined learning environment and a focus on character education. Perhaps most importantly, Friendship schools are led by outstanding educators like Dr. John Pannell at Chamberlain and the nationally renowned Vonnelle Middleton, the chief academic officer.

The dramatic achievement gains of Friendship students deserve closer attention. Friendship has been one of the charters with strong assessment and impact results: Since the schools opened three years ago, they've had an average increase of 85 percent in mathematics and 55 percent in reading scores. The school's Chamberlain Elementary campus opened in fall 1998. The fall Stanford 9 test that year showed that the average student scored in the 27th percentile in reading. These students, after only a few years in the DCPS system, were at extreme risk of educational failure. By spring 2001, reading scores had skyrocketed to the 59th percentile in reading and 62nd in math. The average Chamberlain second grader scored at the 82nd percentile in reading. Students at Chamberlain—right across the street from the Potomac Gardens public housing development—are scoring above national norms, at levels comparable to schools in D.C.'s most affluent neighborhoods.

The FH middle school opened in 1999, and the high school collegiate academy in 2000. There are now a total of three thousand children on four campuses, and there was a waiting list in the fall 2002 of over a thousand children for the elementary school. The high school won a student achievement award in its first year and was significant enough to be named a four-star school, making it the first Edison high school to receive four stars.

Friendship Edison leaders recognize that quality instruction alone is not enough to reach the highest levels of achievement. Their vision is to build a network of partnerships and programs to expand the horizons of their students and to remove barriers to learning. The school's founding partner, Friendship House, provides after-school programs, family literacy programs, and a youth development specialist for the high school. Another invaluable partner is the D.C. Center for Student Support Services. The center has placed three full-time mental health workers in its schools, and has provided training and resources for violence prevention, youth development, and after-school programs.

Friendship students also benefit from partnerships with Hampshire College, Miami University of Ohio, Southeastern University, the Kennedy Center, the Higher Achievement Program, and many others. Another partner is the Reach for Tomorrow Program, which provides opportunities for Friendship students to have summer experiences at the Air Force Academy and the University of San Diego. The school has also entered into a partnership with Northern Virginia Community College that permits their students to begin taking college-level courses for credit in the eleventh and twelfth grades, while providing academic enrichments in lower grade levels.[93]

There is very specific community involvement in what's happening at Friendship House. It is often the case that community members want schools to be successful, but they do not know how to help. FH provides them a voice in what goes on in the process earlier as opposed to later. It also binds parents, teachers, and students to quarterly learning contracts. The three groups sit down together and review progress made in the past quarter. They map out where they want to go in the coming quarter. Each will state what he or she intends to do to assist in the process. Once finished, the three parties sign the contract and that is the instrument by which they are reviewed.

FH has also developed a number of community-specific programs, including a parenting-plus program to teach parents how to be parents. Hense notes that some of the parents in the community have just barely passed childhood themselves. FH teaches them things like what the stages of growth are, that it's not natural for children to sit down or shut up, that children learn by picking things up and taking them apart. FH also offers exercise programs and financial management and housing seminars, teaching community members how to save for and buy a house. Periodically, the organization conducts surveys to find out what other programs community members are interested in.

Like many other D.C. charters, FH's objective is to provide wraparound services. They also are building on the community school model. That is, they have built into their school certain types of social services, including mental health and family counseling and referrals, and a health center in the high school. The high school remains open until

9 P.M., and FH's ultimate goal is to have every school open until 9 P.M. Before- and after-school staff are available through a program called D.C. Kids.

Test scores at Friendship's two elementary campuses, Woodbridge and Chamberlain, have risen faster than scores at 105 out of 106 DCPS elementary schools since 1998 when the school first opened. That is, only one DCPS elementary school has come close to matching Friendship's performance. The Friendship Junior Academy has also outperformed its DCPS peers. The school's Collegiate Academy graduated its first senior class in 2003, a class well prepared for both college and the workforce.

The SEED School

In 1998, I met Eric Adler and Raj Vinnakota for the first time. They had pressed my council staff for weeks for a meeting to discuss their plans to start a residential charter school. For some time I had believed that public school systems around the country should consider opening nurturing, twenty-four-hour residential schools. Unfortunately, given school administrators' problems in running effective six-hour programs, a college prep boarding program was an innovation most school districts could not even attempt.

At first glance, Eric and Raj left me completely underwhelmed! They looked extremely young and probably too naïve to pull off something so difficult to achieve. I thought to myself, "These snot-nosed kids will never be able to make something this big work." A few minutes into our discussion, I became convinced that those two may be the only ones with the vision, energy, and means to effectively start the first residential public charter school in the country—and indeed they have!

The SEED School is a national model and a pioneering educational program based on the recognition that sometimes a child may be better off living in his or her school environment and may have a better opportunity to learn outside the context of home (but still in the community). The program was founded as a pre-collegiate institution both to benefit D.C. youth and to serve as a model that can have an impact on urban education throughout the nation.

Adler and Vinnakota first started the SEED foundation in 1997 with a mission to open college preparatory boarding schools for urban children. Prior to opening the school, the SEED Foundation secured a public charter, raised more than two million dollars in private donations and commitments, and renovated a temporary campus on the site of the Capital Children's Museum. In addition, the Foundation successfully lobbied for three pieces of legislation from the federal and District governments that allocated supplementary funding for residential charter schools. The SEED Public Charter School is financially sustainable on the public funds it receives, now that it has reached its 300-student capacity.[94]

In 1998, the Foundation opened the doors of the SEED Public Charter School, the nation's first urban public boarding school. At SEED, children from difficult circumstances enjoy a secure and nurturing learning environment twenty-four hours a day. The school provides an intensive college preparatory boarding program for seventh through twelfth grades, to children whose challenging life circumstances may otherwise prevent them from fulfilling their academic potential. Over 80 percent of SEED's students are eligible for Title I funding and more than 85 percent come from single-parent families.

Six years later, the SEED school is an oasis set in one of the District's toughest neighborhoods. Unlike most other of the city's charters, SEED has conquered the facilities issues since its 2000 move into the grounds of an abandoned school in Southeast Washington, an economically underserved community from which many of its students come. The rebuilt and renovated school is now situated in a gated lot on a lush stretch of land—complete with its own security staff. SEED's children receive a top-notch education and cultural enrichment program on par with those found at the nation's best college prep schools. They also maintain healthy contact with their families and communities. The school's presence in the students' community increases parental involvement and reinforces SEED's mission of helping children by revitalizing inner cities. The school also has a full-time parent and community-relations coordinator who recruits and works with parents.

Students come to the school for varied reasons: Some are not thriving in their traditional school environments; others need to escape the negative influences of their neighborhoods; yet others come from volatile families. At SEED, these students are all united in their pursuit of academic excellence. They are provided the education, support, and nurturing needed to fulfill their potential. All share the common goal of graduating not only from high school, but from college as well. The overwhelming majority of these students will probably go on to college and/or graduate school.

SEED students maintain a rigorous schedule ten months a year, during which they spend one long weekend a month with their families. Students attend classes from 8 A.M. to 4 P.M. Monday through Friday. In the afternoons, they enjoy a variety of recreational activities, including volleyball, flag football, tennis, basketball, soccer, drama, dance, art, and more. After dinner, staff and volunteers work with the students on homework and to review material covered in classes. On Saturdays and Sundays, students take part in field trips, cultural excursions, and community service. Academic and boarding faculty are available at all times to answer questions or to provide further information and insight.

SEED students have made great academic and personal strides just a few short years into the program. Previously "difficult" and academically challenged students are energized about school. They are involved in science, social studies, computers, photography and acting. A majority of children plan to attend college and have developed ambitious goals and aspirations.

Students progressing through the SEED program demonstrate significant intellectual and social advancement. Independent evaluations of the school have indicated that students have made greater than one-year academic gains in each school year. In addition the campus atmosphere has notably increased students' social skills and self-esteem and significantly lowered their exposure to high-risk behaviors. For example, only 3 percent of SEED students have used cigarettes, compared to 70.4 percent of same-aged, non-SEED school, D.C. children.

SEED's ninth-grade "gate" is a pioneering concept in education. The school offers a skills-based middle school program with no grade expectations or expected timelines. This enables each student to fully prepare, both socially and academically, for SEED's upper school college preparatory program. At the end of the eighth grade, each student must have completed the requirements for the ninth-grade gate in order to be admitted into SEED's college preparatory upper-school program. The gate is composed of both academic and social skills that are critical for the student's ability to focus on social and academic preparation for college.

SEED's mission—to prepare its students both academically and socially for entrance success in college—permeates all aspects of its residential and academic program. College is a fundamental component of both its academic and boarding programs. For example, all residential halls in the dormitories are named after colleges (e.g., Princeton, Swarthmore, Howard, West Point, and University of Maryland houses).

Since opening the school, SEED has raised more than twenty-two million dollars, and renovated and built the school's permanent campus. Financial supporters of SEED include Donald and Ann Brown, Melvin and Ryna Cohen, Morris & Gwendolyn Cafritz Foundation, and George Preston Marshall Foundation. The school has developed strong relationships with local business leaders, educators, and politicians. Many community leaders sit on SEED's board and advise the school on a range of strategic and tactical issues.

The Cesar Chavez School

With its unique emphasis on public policy, Cesar Chavez Public Charter High School has turned out to be one of D.C.'s most innovative charters. Cesar Chavez is a college preparatory high school dedicated to preparing young people to seek reform and progress by influencing public policies that affect their communities. The school opened in September 1998 with a class of sixty ninth-graders and has been adding a grade level each year. In the 2001–02 school year, Chavez reached full capacity with 240 ninth through twelfth graders.[95] Drawing on the vast policy resources in the District of Columbia, Chavez challenges students with a rigorous curriculum that fosters citizenship and prepares them to excel in college and life. The school uses public policy themes to guide instruction and provides students direct experience with organizations working in the public interest.[96]

Many of the high school's students had never set foot in the White House or on Capitol Hill prior to attending Chavez. The school teaches its students how to gain access to local and national leaders, and assists them in understanding their power to influence policy. A full-time public policy director works with the teaching faculty to incorporate public policy themes and activities into the curriculum. Activities include field trips, workshops, training and activities, public policy fellowships, lobby training and lobby days, community service projects, and "public policy capstones," a series of press conferences and public presentations by students on various topics of import, based on their own research and findings. Students are also required to prepare a senior thesis prior to graduation. Volunteer students from Howard

University and Georgetown's Public Policy Institute often take part in the high school's policy activities.

The Chavez student body, which is 60 percent African American and 40 percent Hispanic, also benefits from unique partnerships rarely found in traditional public schools. For example, Chavez has a partnership with Cornell University, which affords several students an opportunity to visit the school during spring break. Trinity University hosts a four-day college summit in the summer for as many as fifteen Chavez juniors. In 2001, several male students traveled to Atlanta to participate in the fifteenth annual Conference of 100 Black Men of America, Inc. Also that year, five Chavez juniors traveled to Brazil with the Partners of Americas to participate in a two-week conflict resolution-oriented cultural exchange program.[97]

Chavez's principal and founder, Irasema Salcido, was formerly part of the District's public schools. She has emerged as a dynamic and high-profile charter school principal who had the vision of running a school with a public policy emphasis independent of bureaucratic entanglements.

According to Ms. Salcido, success requires perseverance and commitment:

> You see how much students will struggle because they don't have the skills to write the essay or to do the thesis. We saw this all in the context of their previous experiences. They were not held to high standards and now they are in an environment where they have to meet these rigorous requirements. There is some unfairness to that because these kids should have been prepared, but they were not and now they have to do the extra work and be frustrated and feel like they're not up to the challenge. It's also a challenge for us. It tested our beliefs and many times we felt like we might have to give up, but we demanded and expected, and for the most part, we got what we were asking for.[98]

And the persistence is paying off. Chavez's spring 2001 Stanford 9 test results reveal prominent gains. Eleventh graders at Chavez distinguished themselves at the District and national levels on all content clusters, and the high school's sophomores outperformed District students on all clusters.[99]

According to Nelson Smith, former executive director of the District of Columbia Public Charter School Board, Chavez's success is due to the fact that its students are in "an environment that maximizes their ability to learn. Yes, there should be a core curriculum, but it doesn't have to be uniform and the charter model gives you different ways of getting important facts and knowledge to the kids."

Carlos Rosario School

The Carlos Rosario International Public Charter School is not a conventional school by any definition. First of all, it primarily serves adults, with students ranging in age from sixteen to eighty. The school's mission emphasizes assisting immigrant and indigent populations. Its students are mainly members of the non-English speaking immigrant communities in the District. The students come for many reasons: They come to gain English language skills in classes structured to follow the school's comprehensive ESL curriculum for adult learners, developed by expert faculty with the help of the Center for Applied Linguistics. They come to obtain high school diplomas through the school's GED courses. They come to gain computer literacy skills. And many come for the citizenship classes—to become better American citizens.[100]

In 1970, Carlos Manuel Rosario established the Program of English Instruction for Latin Americans (PEILA) in the Latino barrio on Irving Street in Northwest Washington. Two years later, Sonia Guiterriez, now the school's principal, became the program director. Under Ms. Guiterriez's leadership, the school expanded and merged with the Americanization School in 1978. The resulting institution operated under the auspices of D.C. Public School's Division of Adult and Continuing Education, and relocated to the Gordon Junior High School building in Georgetown. Eventually renamed the Carlos Rosario Adult Education Center in honor of its founder, the program grew to provide approximately four thousand students per year with comprehensive language and vocational training and supportive services.

From 1970 to 1996, the Carlos Rosario Center graduated over fifty thousand "new Americans" who joined the workforce and established themselves as a new generation of naturalized citizens in the nation's capital. The Center won numerous awards for its programs and services, including recognition by the U.S. Department of Education and by the National School Board Association for excellence in adult education.[101]

Sonia Guiterriez is an attractive slip of a woman—five foot three inches of pure energy. Her devotion to her school is evident as she tells the story of the school's conversion to a charter. In 1996, amidst the city's financial crisis, the city administration decided to eliminate certain schools because many of them were filled only to half capacity. Carlos Rosario was filled to capacity and always had been. At the time, it was serving as a national model and its program had been duplicated in seven different cities. The school had also been observed by Korea and Germany as a possible model for their adult learning needs. On the eve of the announcements of the closings, the city promised Ms. Guiterriez that Rosario was safe from the cutbacks. But the next day the axe fell, and school administrators were told that the city was going to eliminate adult education altogether. More than four thousand students were left with no alternative program to continue their ESL and vocational courses. Politics had won the battle, but Rosario administrators were intent on winning the war.

The school was officially shut down in June 1996. Determined to continue the services so vital to the success of the immigrant community, Ms. Guiterriez and former staff members raised local foundation money to re-establish the school as an independent, non-profit learning center. By April 1997, they were able to open a small school in a basement in Chinatown with sixty-five students being taught by three part-time teachers. In November 1997, the school leaders applied for a charter and were still seeking seed funding from several foundations.

According to Sonia: "In the traditional system, there almost seems to be a prejudice against adult education, and that makes it much harder to have a credible program. The charter school movement elevates the adult education issue to the level it should be by emphasizing lifelong learning and adult education. It acknowledges that parents are affecting the children, and it permits us to focus on the parents."

One of the major initial hurdles in the application for charter status as an adult education center was the absence of an adult education funding formula. Adult education had not originally been contemplated under the charter school design. Working with the school, I introduced and passed council legislation to fit the school's needs. By fall 1997, the school had obtained its charter, becoming the first adult charter school in the nation. Carlos Rosario opened its doors the following September at four different locations, with a total of four hundred students.

The program's mission also included sixteen-year-olds who by all measures were considered "failures and troublemakers" and who with the blessings of their middle and high school principals were sent to Rosario to learn English and obtain their GEDs. In the subsequent five years, Rosario has met and surpassed its target new enrollment rate of eight hundred students. Currently the school is attended by roughly twelve hundred students per year, with many more on the waiting list.

The Carlos Rosario School is unique in that it not only provides its students with excellent classes, but it also has a holistic approach to learning. The school's administrators realize that in order for their educational efforts to be successful, they must also meet the needs of the whole person. So they provide supportive services to their students with a highly qualified team of bilingual counselors and staff. This team offers counseling as well as other related and unrelated assistance: helping students with taxes, finding childcare or a better job; raising money for college scholarships; getting students into local colleges; and referring students to other local service providers.

A visit to the Rosario school is a trip to another land. The corridors are frequented by faces from every country, with many of Hispanic origin. Spanish words are volleyed from every angle. Even the English spoken in these halls is flavored with Spanish timbre. The school administration is simple: Rosario operates under one executive director, several assistant directors, and a board of trustees. Decisions are made and implemented without wasting time.

Areas of instruction are tailored to serve the needs of its student body: literacy, English as a Second Language, GED, EL/civics, citizenship, computer-assisted instruction, and workplace computer training are the school's main offerings. The school's curriculum is revised constantly. The school emphasizes measuring impact and has received substantial funding for assessments from the Charter School Resource Center. Teachers work with various assessment consultants from the Resource Center to develop and conduct pre- and post-tests. Most Rosario students perform exceedingly well. The school also conducts frequent needs assessments to determine its students' learning needs.

The school has a strict policy against social promotions. It uses a student progress summary as a criterion for deciding whether students will be promoted. Because Rosario students are adults who are classified as non-English proficient, testing is based on curriculum objectives. Portfolios are kept on file for each student and used as one of several indicators of success or failure. Teachers also consider a needs assessment, a goal sheet setting out the individual's short- and long-term goals, sample job applications, sample resumes, quizzes, and other relevant material. The portfolios are used to track students' progress from beginning to end—one of Rosario's charter mandates. The local tests are all criterion-referenced and developed by teachers.

The school's norm-referenced testing is based on the Comprehensive Assessment System of Adult Students (CASAS), which is used by almost all adult education systems in the country. CASAS reflects performance skills that are aligned with the role maps of the Equipped for the Future guidelines published by the U.S. Department of Labor. Rosario itself has positively surpassed expectations on every single evaluation. Passing rates are high, and each year a number of Rosario students enroll in college.

Carlos Rosario requires all of its teachers to be certified. The school's teachers receive only one-year "at-will" contracts, subject to a serious system of evaluations used as a tool to improve instructional delivery in the classroom. All teachers are given the opportunity to take courses in adult education, linguistics, and ESL in order to meet the local education agency's credentialing requirements. School administrators note that students tend to be teachers' best evaluators. In renewing teacher contracts, evaluators consider state objectives and assessment tools. A conference is held between the teacher and the evaluator in which the teacher's performance in the past year is reviewed. In general, teachers are subject to observations, student evaluations, and the outcome of the school board on assessment tools. "If teachers are not performing, with all due respect, they are not renewed!"

The school consistently has attracted an impressive pool of talented teachers. Sonia Guiterriez reasons that if a school has good programs and high standards, it will attract good teachers. The principal is also important. He or she can be demanding and exacting, but must have vision.

The school's immediate and larger community has certainly felt its impact. Rosario students are gaining better, higher paying jobs, contributing to the tax base, buying homes, and joining the ranks of middle-class consumers who help drive the local economy.

Several independent audits are conducted throughout the year, perusing all accounts payable and receivable receipts, and ensuring the direct benefits of per-capita allocations to students. A full-time equivalent (FTE) formula is used to report enrollment and attendance, which is taken daily. The school reports to the charter board, its board of trustees, and faculty and staff on a monthly basis. In addition, there are regular meetings with the student government and faculty. In each financial program and enrollment audit, the Carlos Rosario School has been rated "outstanding." The school has also been acknowledged at the Public Charter School Resource Center MAC awards. One of Rosario's star students, Gerry Hernandez, was selected as the MAC Awards Student of the Year in 1999, and the school was recognized as the School with the Greatest Student Satisfaction in both 2000 and 2001.

The school has developed a national reputation. With the assistance of the Charter School Resource Center and the Center for Applied Linguistics, the school's accountability plan includes objectives mandated by the Secretary's Commission on Achieving Necessary Skills (SCANS) and the English as a Second Language (ESOL) Standards. Two summer institutes have been conducted with the full participation of teachers to develop the performance-based curriculum. These were also included in the accountability plan.

Sonia Guiterriez has also helped the school establish strong bonds with local agencies and public officials. The Office of Latino Affairs, the Ethiopian Community Center, the Chinese Community, the Council of Hispanic Agencies, and many others interact and collaborate with Rosario on various issues and projects. Also, the relationship between the school and the local government is non-confrontational and mutually supportive.

One of the tenets of the school's philosophy and mission is that each student will give back to the community what he or she has received. The school's philosophy is that in order to succeed as a student, one must be fully integrated in city life and involved in civic duties and responsibilities. Indeed, citizenship is one of Rosario's course offerings. Once students are naturalized, they register to vote in local and federal elections.

One of the school's ongoing problems has been the facilities issue. Since its inception, the school has moved several times—from Chinatown to Adams Morgan and back. Carlos Rosario currently occupies six separate sites and includes a day and evening program. The school leaders negotiated a deal with the city to renovate an old school. The renovation will be completed by January 2004, at which time all six sites will move to the new building.

In all, over fifty thousand students have passed through the Carlos Rosario School's doors over the past thirty years. Many have become U.S. citizens, bought homes, and have a new generation of children under their wings. They have learned English and integrated themselves into mainstream society. These students include bankers, insurance agents, doctors, and lawyers.

The Maya Angelou School

My true, honest, moral belief is that if anybody understood the level of emotional and academic needs kids come to us with, we would be having a completely different conversation about education.

—David Domenici, co-founder
of Maya Angelou School[102]

David Domenici and James Forman, Jr., co-founders of the Maya Angelou Public Charter School (MAPCS), established the school to help provide opportunities for youth they had encountered in the juvenile justice system. Their brainchild, MAPCS, began with twenty students in 1997.

Maya Angelou Public Charter School is a comprehensive charter school for at-risk and court-involved teens in the District. Students—many of whom have been in the juvenile justice system—are involved in activities year round, up to 10.5 hours per day during the school year, and between six and eight hours per day during the summer break.

The Angelou School's curriculum is anything but standard. With average class sizes of about eight, all students are required to take math, social studies, technology, science, and English. Electives include photography, theater, drama, and technology offerings such as web design and hardware repair. Many of the school's students are dropouts, and most read and write at an elementary-school level. Those in need of extra assistance receive intensive literacy instruction one-on-one or in pairs, and all students participate in evening tutoring programs four nights a week. All of Angelou's classes use technology, including computers and the Internet.

Two critical factors about Maya Angelou stand out:

The school works with some of the most hard-to-reach kids. Most Maya Angelou students did not succeed in traditional school settings. Many had been arrested or had dropped out of school before coming to Maya Angelou. They did not participate in mainstream after-school and youth activities. Simply put, the program strives to reach kids who are headed for lives of marginal employment and intermittent incarceration. Once they've been "reached" by school staff, there is an attempt to provide them with the skills and resources they need to achieve their dreams.

The school produces excellent outcomes. On average, Maya Angelou graduates improve their standardized test scores, grades, and attendance significantly while they are at the school. Over 70 percent of Angelou graduates enroll in college. Recent alumni are attending schools including Spelman College, Trinity College, St. Mary's College, Morgan State University, the University of Delaware, and Hollins University, as well as community colleges in D.C. and Maryland.

Students are achieving at these levels in spite of many coming to MAPCS without having attended school in the previous year, over 90 percent having grown up in poverty, over 40 percent having been involved in the court system and nearly 50 percent having special needs.[103]

In 2001, the Angelou School had sixty-five students between the ages of fourteen and nineteen, twelve teachers, and three social workers. According to Domenici, "The single most valuable input in our school is loving or hugging the kids." They have good teachers, most of whom came to MAPCS to work for a non-profit, hoping to make a difference. MAPCS owns its building and is attempting to find a long-term solution for a gym, perhaps by developing a gym jointly with the Boys and Girls Club or by forming another creative sharing relationship. The school has found it difficult to form an institutional level of cooperation with the public elementary school directly across the street, even though that school does not use its gym when MAPCS would need it.

Angelou's brilliance is possibly in its common-sense simplicity. The school leaders find that they have to be able to respond quickly to issues as they come up. For example, they have developed a limited boarding capacity, with a residential wing that houses eight boys. This wing was created in direct response to some students' problems with unsuitable home environments.[104]

Although the charter school concept has served MAPCS well, it was not the driving force behind the school's start. Founders Forman and Domenici noticed that a group of children were not participating in summer jobs or mentoring programs. The then-alternative schools were merely serving as warehouses rather than educational facilities. The alternative, schools such as Hamilton, were schools of last resort. Forman and Domenici felt that this set kids up for a life without a decent chance of success.

MAPCS leaders are proponents of longer school days and school years. Their school day extends until 8 P.M. and does not start until 11 A.M. on Wednesday to accommodate students' parole meetings. The school has two built-in vocational programs in culinary arts and technology. Other programs range from substance abuse prevention to surviving abusive relationships. They also teach daily life skills, including a forced savings program to help students invest and to teach financial responsibility.

So many MAPCS students are so far behind that the school's primary goal is to help these young people reach basic levels. The school has set up literacy classes to address the fact that some of the school's students cannot read. On the other hand, some MAPCS students are showing exceptional academic potential, and have graduated and gone on to junior college. The school conducts assessments at both entrance and graduation, and measures both qualitative and quantitative issues.

Maya Angelou receives a good deal of community support. It receives college interns and law students each summer. During the school year, fifty volunteers tutor kids during study hall every night. A majority of school volunteers tend to be African American, which school leaders consider important because a majority of students are African American. Partners include the Urban League, Outward Bound, Cornell University's pre-college program, and Living Stages, which helps with an arts program. The level of cooperation from the students' families varies. A third of the parents never come to the school.

The school's response time to emergencies is reasonably quick. The students remain at high risk. Traditional public schools have not adjusted to the reality of day-to-day pressures for these kids. MAPCS has the creativity and flexibility to do what they need to do to help the children.

The school is 80 percent publicly funded. It does not have a development director, but raises private money for its various programs. By the time the school year starts, the school has generally done a good assessment so that it receives special education dollars as well. MAPCS is not meeting many D.C. Public School standards, "partly because some of them are inane and partly because some of them MAPCS students cannot meet." But Angelou is trying something different: the school is spending $20,000 to $25,000 per child (more than double what public schools spend) to see where they end up in five years. If it works, they reason, they can say to the public and private sectors that here we have children who were expected to end up marginalized or incarcerated, who started out reading at fifth-grade levels, but who now can hold full-time jobs and understand long-term commitments.

The Principle of Mobilizing Collective Capacity: An Interview with Community Academy's Kent Amos

The success of the District's charters is due in no small part to the schools' many extraordinary leaders. Examples include Thomas Stewart, the first principal of the SEED School, who endeared himself to parents and community leaders from the very beginning. His involvement in the SEED experiment was important particularly since the two founders of the SEED school did not hail from the community they served. Another example, Donald Hense, is a well-known black male figure in the District who, as the head of the Friendship House, has been involved in charitable community causes for years. Without his involvement as the point person for the Edison schools, it would have been much more difficult for Edison to gain traction in the city. In effect, Donald Hense is the face of the Friendship Edison schools in D.C.

Kent Amos, a former Xerox executive, has a longstanding reputation in the community as a man who has dedicated his life to the city's needy children. When Kent decided to pursue a charter school through the Community Academy, it was almost assumed that the school would be nurturing and enriching for children and that it would be competently run, largely because of Kent's involvement. In fact, all of those expectations have been realized and surpassed.

I do not believe that only African American teachers can be effective with black students. It is important, however, for urban minority students to have positive role models in their lives who look like them, especially in a school setting. By featuring some of these individuals, our most successful charter schools reflect the diversity in the community and the image that many parents want to have their children exposed to.

The first thing that got my attention about Kent Amos was his passion for children. I knew he had been an executive at Xerox, and that he and his wife had adopted several children and taken in countless others. It wasn't until I spoke to him that I began to appreciate the depths of his passion. I knew of him through my involvement with the community but I got to know him better once I got elected. He always saw the need for the city to make a stronger commitment to children. When charter school legislation passed, we met extensively and talked about the community hub concept. That's when he first shared with me his vision of the community hub campus. I sat with him one afternoon to discuss leadership:

> The concept of leadership is an art and therefore it can be learned as a craft. I have gone through the learning process in a number of different systems to become who I am today. I learned at officer candidates' school in the army that leadership is the art of deploying people to follow your directions willingly. I have followed this principle in life and added an element: you have to get people to believe first and foremost in you, the person, or they won't follow you willingly. They can believe in the office you hold and follow you because of that office, but that's different from *willingly*. You get different results between people who do things because they want to and those who have to. We strive to educate people so that they buy into the collective vision of where we're going.

I was in the army on full active duty in Vietnam. When I came back from duty, I went to work for Xerox as an entry-level sales representative. On my first assignment, I was number one in sales in the whole country; in the second assignment I was in the top five percent; and in my third, I set a sales record for the product line. In seven years, I was a vice president at the company—the youngest, the fastest, and the first African American [to start out at entry level and reach vice presidency]. Through all of that I was continually going to class and being trained for management.

At some point I realized that I had a wealth of experience; I had honed my craft; and I understood my strengths and weaknesses over a variety of venues and under different circumstances. I also had a commitment to the city and wanted to bring that power and capacity home; to use it to effect transformation in a city that made it possible for me to be who I am.

One question that came about in my personal life at that point was, where would my wife and I put our own children in school? Because I had done well financially, I had a lot of options available to me. The last one anyone expected me to choose was D.C. public schools. But my mother had taught for thirty-two years in D.C. public schools. My father, who was an attorney, had graduated from a D.C. public school. My grandfather had met my grandmother at a D.C. public school where he was a teacher and taught for forty-seven years. Even my great-grandfather had come out of DCPS. The notion that I would put my kids anywhere else was alien to me.

I understood the issues associated with the system, but systems survive because of the people who support the system. In D.C., people who had the means withdrew those means from the public system when they withdrew their children. And when they left, they took their capacity with them. That left the urban-centered brown and black schools lacking the resources I had had available to me when I attended them.

I decided to do something different: I would send my

kids to DCPS and put the resources of my company into the system. So for five years we had a summer youth investment program, which in its heyday enrolled seven hundred kids. We paid to build an entire computer center in a public high school. And we invested in the schools.

And when my children came home with their school friends—kids who could use what we had as a family—we didn't turn our backs on them, either. My tradition has taught me that it's the collective capacity—not individual capacity—that raises children. My parents—as well off as they were—didn't raise me alone. There was "Uncle" Joe who sat on the front stoop of my building; Mrs. Stokes who made sure that if someone did something wrong, that information got home; Mrs. Pride; Shiloh Baptist Church; my second grade teacher . . .

That collective experience was now mine to do something with. Just like I could have avoided public schools, I could have avoided that too, but that would have been wrong. I would not have paid back the debt that I owed for those who sacrificed for me to do what I ended up doing. I hadn't created the opportunities for myself—my community and family had. And that's what drives me: the recognition that life is fleeting. That in the context of humanity, I am an "instant." Louis Farrakhan once told me that it makes more sense to support the infinite, rather than the finite. I chose to adopt that as a philosophy of life.

There was one year where several of my children's school friends died from a variety of causes that children should not be dying from. My wife and I set out to make sure that the children's sacrifice was not in vain. I had to use the full capacity given me to solve the problem of children in pain—pain associated with living in poverty, deprivation, and an anonymous life of ignorance.

We established the Urban Family Institute and dedicated it to the process of providing children and their families with pathways of possibility and joy. Our first effort was around the notion called Kid's House. The question we asked was: If one is going to be a successful adult, what system has to be applied to create a pathway for this to happen? It's a 24–7/365/20 proposition—that is, 24 hours a day for 7 days a week for 365 days a year for over 20 years.

People don't "arrive" in places by themselves. They've been through a host of systems: a family system (regardless of what the construct was); community systems (faith-based, forced or volunteer; schooling systems; and perhaps others); neighborhood systems; and government systems. All of these systems have been prepositioned before you came along. You designed none of them for yourself. Their collective input to you produced you.

We set out to find the 24–7/365/20 paradigm scaled to bring all children through. The answer to this was far easier when I was a child in the city. In those days we lived in the remnants of tribes because we were ethnically isolated, and the black community was diverse. We all went to the same schools, commercial districts, and recreation places. That was a good thing because you were able to interact with various elements: You were uplifted by those who were more positive and were able to reject others.

Today we live based on the price point of houses. You limit your perspective to the people who live in your neighborhood which was often chosen according to the price a house dictates. You then also do your commerce associated with your level of income. You shop in places that are specific to your economic power. This dynamic begins to "verticalize" our society whereas when we were children, we had horizontal societies.

We designed Kid's House around the notion of "rehorizontalizing" the society so that children and their families see each other in the larger context of a family of humanity. The family of humanity is still rich in capacity that some children never see. Kid's House is now in twenty-two states in all kinds of venues: Boys and Girls Clubs, prisons, the YMCA. They're all locally partnered.

In the process of building that continuum for children, we began to recognize that many adults needed support as well. We set out to design a system around adult development, the Urban Family University.

The Community Academy was really our third initiative. The school grew out of our work in a very holistic way. We founded it because we needed a place where all of this development could take place—a community center where you can develop during the school day and then after the school day. We found the best talent we could find. We hired and gave their due to really smart and talented people, wherever they come from. It wasn't a matter of age, but a question of competencies. We have people who go the extra mile to see that others succeed.

We have sought out not only competent people, but competent *processes*. There are a number of different curricula out there, and we take the best of each. We examine various after-school components, and we take the best of those. We invested two million dollars over two years in after-school curriculum development. It is one of the best in the country.

We brought in capacity and contacts, and developed partnerships. We have a stellar board at the school. And that's the beauty of what we're doing: we are using our collective capacity—not the individual power—to make us whatever we are. I believe very strongly in leadership and therefore whatever leadership I provide is very important—I'm not trying to discount its importance—but at the end of the day it's all about the collective capacity and everyone working toward the common goal.

Our initial charter was large because the idea was to affect the whole community that we lived and worked in. If you can reach a critical mass of that size, you can certainly influence how things are done in the larger context. If it was not for the charter movement, school reform as we see it today would not have happened. And the fact is that they still do not use us as they should.

The relationship between charter and public schools is that we are of the same construct but not of the same mind. The public school leadership is not actively resisting the charter movement, but they do not value it to the level they should. And that is tragic. There are many things that charters could be used effectively for, if we operated cooperatively: testing conceptual frameworks and programmatic thrust; isolating requirements that cannot be accommodated in the bigger system; specialization of programs.

Some of these things are happening to a lesser extent, but they are not planned or orchestrated. So rather than maximum benefits, you have minimal effectiveness. We owe our children more than that. Our children deserve more than "incremental better." We certainly have the collective capacity to be significantly better. And the children are the ones who are paying the price. There is too much self-interest. Self-interest is important, but when it competes with the broader interest, you have failed.

I would work diligently with our political leadership (both the mayor and city council) to build a cabinet of officers that deal with the development processes of human beings to meet regularly to design our process for 24 hours a day; 7 days a week; 365 days a year. You can't get where you are going unless you know where you are going. The mayor has a citywide plan, and one of them is a human development subset. The UDC leadership, the DCPS and charter leadership, health and human services, and recreation—all these groups should be consciously designing the 24-7/365 and figuring out which functions should be handled by which agency. Before any action is taken, there must be an intellectual exercise that shapes the outcome. In some communities, school must stay open—as a minimum proposition—fourteen hours a day. In every school quadrant, there should be certain government services that build out the paradigm of development.

When the school system was created two hundred years ago, the paradigm was one of an agrarian culture. The nine to three school day is the descendant of an agrarian world. There was a time when children had to be in the fields in the morning and at home in the evenings for planting and pulling. That's also why children didn't attend school in the summertime. The problem is that we've built a paradigm that no one wants to change. Even assuming that because of the demands of our society we can't get there immediately, we need to put in place the pathways to the product we are seeking by working with architects, engineers, and planners who think through, plan, and then go on to create.

Effective Teachers; Phenomenal Schools:
An Interview with the SEED School's Brandon Lloyd

Effective teachers like Brandon Lloyd represent a new breed that has surfaced with the burgeoning charters: unlimited in perspective, unfettered by tradition, unshackled by bureaucracy.[105] At one time, I was a strong believer in the requirement for teacher certification. I no longer feel as adamant about this issue. Our charter and private schools have demonstrated that some uncertified teachers may be as qualified and exceptional as any other teacher.

Felix "Brandon" Lloyd is one of SEED's star teachers: a suave young man who at first glance looks more GQ than IQ. Minutes after meeting him, he will impress you with his intelligence and profound insights about children, their psyches, and how they learn best. Prior to the SEED school, Brandon's teaching experience was . . . zero! He majored in African American studies and dramatic writing at Syracuse University in upstate New York and graduated in 1998. Before that, he spent seven years in D.C. public schools (grades K–6) and six years in military school (grades 7–12).

During his last year at Syracuse, Brandon reflected on what he wanted to do with his life. The one thing he knew was that he had always wanted to be a writer. And so he applied to eight or nine of the best creative writing programs in the country. He was rejected by everyone—an admittedly humbling and frightening experience. Left with little choice, he decided to come back to D.C.. He took a summer job teaching drama and literary arts to children in recreation centers in southeast D.C. It was only a six- to eight-week program and a totally different and casual teaching atmosphere. At the end of the summer, he received a call asking if he was interested in being a resident assistant at SEED. Reluctantly and only after some time, he returned the call:

> Frankly I went in for the interview thinking it would give me time to write. At the interview they asked if I could also

teach social studies. I said, sure I could! A week later I was teaching social studies for the first time: no textbook and no concept of what it was like to be a teacher—which was actually valuable. They were seventh graders and I wasn't really scared of the kids but I definitely was afraid of failure. To put it mildly, I was in a gray space but the kids didn't know it.

From then on I worked really hard and stayed up all kinds of nights. I learned as I went along. It was the first day of school, and the whole school was new. It was a discovery process for me. Some of the kids were excited that I gave out nicknames to kids and stood up in class. That year I formed great relationships with the kids! A turning point was the drama production that we did in the spring where the kids worked really hard. (Since the kids lived there, I also ran a drama program called Seed Squared in the evenings.)

The year ended, and within the school they named me teacher of the year. But there were only five teachers that first year, and I was a young guy who worked really hard! I guess everyone loved that. My second year there was pretty much the same process. I was still involved in a process of discovery. At the end of the year I was again named teacher of the year. That year I won an award for major achievements in charters (the MAC awards). In year three, I was promoted to department head for social studies [at twenty-four]. That's when I started to have a body of knowledge and experience. I was nominated for teacher of the year again, and actually won the MAC Awards' Teacher of the Year in the spring.

I work extremely hard. I'm up late most of the nights, and I like what I do. I think I was a good student with good teachers, and I went to good schools. I didn't like school while I was there, but I can appreciate it now. We ran a good program without having a master's degree and experience in a classroom or shadowing somebody. Instead, I referred to my own school experiences, and what it was like for me to get the *A*'s that I got as a student, and which teachers made the most sense.

What are my methods? I believe in giving students a

voice and bringing excitement to the classroom. I believe in not only having a lot of energy and being open to ideas but in bringing things down to a level for the kids; it still elevates them intellectually. I'll call a kid by a nickname. For example Patrice Murphy becomes PM Sunshine. Every kid has one and everyone has "aka" names. I have a secret handshake with the kids. At the same time, we are talking about the Constitution and principles of democracy and using real life examples to teach.

You can't underestimate the fact that most of my children are black and I'm black. They're young and I'm young. For the boys that's very important because of the father-figure issue. For me, when I was in elementary school all of my teachers were older and female. And my father was not extremely present. All that said, I have no doubt that I can go into a classroom of fifteen-year-old white kids in the suburbs and have success there as well. I walk into a classroom and hold them to a certain standard and that's where I operate from.

There are times when the kids may want to "over-identify" with me. [Now I'm dean of students.] When I was twenty-two, I had to let the kids know that even though I was young, I was not their best friend, although I was into being their best friend. I was not operating around that box. That's something I'm proud of too.

I would be interested in teaching in a public school to see if I could have success in terms of what I'd be comfortable with. Whether I could do some of the things we've been able to do. But I'm absolutely fine with where I am! There are clear differences on paper. I share a higher level of intimacy with the kids, and that benefits all parties. I think my school is safer than the perception I have of these other public schools, and the kids feel like they're part of something special. They're part of a private culture and are expected to achieve as a special group.

In terms of assessment results, we did at best the same as most D.C. schools in the first two years. Last year and this year, we had very dramatic gains in math and did well in English. In two years, there'll be a tremendous separation. There are still baby steps, and many things are still happening for the first time. We held a second town hall meeting today for teachers, administrators, support staff ,and students. The theme of this one was success in school. We're going to have one at the beginning of every month.

Eric and Raj (the SEED School founders) got Microsoft to choose two schools—one in Washington State and another in Washington, D.C.—and got us with one another. Microsoft came to visit the school. Bill Gates came to the school: "You don't know what to expect but the unexpected and that's all you can ask for." Along with the other school, we got computers, cameras, printers, and lots of other equipment. My social studies class joined with a science classroom. The teacher and I met face to face, and came up with our program over the summer. Microsoft flew the other teacher and me to Seattle to the Microsoft campus. We had a rental car and a budget . . . they gave us a lot of space. Overall, it was a very good time.

At some point we decided to leave Microsoft's campus. This other teacher was a white guy in his forties. He took me to Mt. St. Helen's, forests, and mountains . . . Eventually we came up with the idea of the kids creating a country. We named it "Generation I-land." The scenario was that the president had issued an executive order for proposals on how to colonize this island. Sixteen students in my class and twenty-five in his participated.

During the process of discovery, we made mistakes and we learned things. We were amazed at how the kids could do different things. They came up with different aspects of this country including flag, bills of rights, energy plants, distribution of power, national animal, and memorials. We'd go on field trips that were related to where we were in the project. For example, we went to the National Zoo and the Smithsonian.

In January, we started off with a Black History Month play. I got a bunch of monologues and scenes from works such as *The Color Purple* and *Colored Girls Who've Considered Suicide, The Bluest Eye,* and *Song of Solomon.* There were thirty-two scenes spanning an hour and half. Of the forty kids in the whole school, all but three were involved. There was a lot of energy and excitement around the play. There was a community theme. The parents were helping with the costumes. All the kids were so excited. The night of the show, they gave me roses and a book with pictures of us preparing for the play, along with notes from each of the children. It was incredible and made me think that I could teach forever. I gave a whole lot of myself for that play. I think I learned the most about how kids learn and what they care about and how to interact with them.

When I first met the kids, most of them had attitude and weren't excited about doing much or learning much. But during this play they got excited. They would rehearse, and mess up, and giggle, and laugh. They worked the hardest I'd ever seen them work. At the end I gave all the kids dog tags with their nicknames. It was tremendous.

Every year there is one little girl who gives me the blues for whatever reason. She decides to be "Anti-Mr. Lloyd." That first year there was this one little girl. I would dread the class and it got to the point where I would start the day by asking her if she was having a good or bad day. If it was a bad day, I would leave her alone, but I stayed on her. She was testing the new guy—the guy everyone loved. Her deal was that she always had stuff going on at home—nothing in particular. Her mother was addicted to something—a substance abuser of some sort—and was only sporadically involved. There wasn't a father that I knew of. That year, on her birthday, she was crying and sitting by the window. I took her to Ruby Tuesday's and we had a great time. I realized how successful I had been in the second year when one day she was walking behind me. I hadn't even seen her. She tapped me on the shoulder and said, "Mr. Lloyd, I respect you a lot. You let me know if anyone messes with you this year!"

With the boys, I would play basketball. During my first year, there was a little boy named Tim. He called himself BJ as in Brandon Junior. He had a father and a very active mother, but this kid walked like me, talked like me, and adopted all my mannerisms. He's done very well in school. He's on the student government at school and almost my height. I think most of these kids will probably go off to college. We have a lot who will go to community college, but the school mission is to send kids to Historically Black Colleges and Ivy Leagues. I think there are so many resources dedicated to these children that a large number of them probably will go to college. Ten to twenty years from now, we'll see assessment numbers that are really based on substantive work. We're not there yet, but this year more than ever.

We've had a lot of turnover: we've had two headmasters and three residential directors. Eric and Raj are good fundraisers. They've created a school that no one has created before. There are no footprints to follow. When that happens, every once in a while you step in quicksand, and every year you have a better idea of what it is you need. We've had high turnover in general. Some just got tired. Others moved on to good things: our science teacher went off to graduate school at Oxford. Many of our people were hired away. People have tremendous resumes and interests, and they're bound to go a lot of places. They can't be held in one location.

The schools and leaders profiled in this chapter are proof that freed from traditional public school regulations and focused on the goal of enhancing scores, public schools and their staffs are able to push their students toward higher achievement. The advantage of a more creative educational institution that is not rigid in terms of hours or course offerings and which has a collaborative relationship with other government agencies is that teachers are able to spend more quality time with children. They are able to come to more realistic assessments of what children's needs are and have resources at their disposal to address those needs without battling bureaucracy.

The essence of the charter school and choice movements is the inherent understanding that one-size-fits-all does not work in the complex fabric of today's society. Traditional public education has failed to understand that the approach to learning those core subjects may differ, and how you engage and excite a child with respect to learning varies.

Therefore in many ways charter schools represent a direct frontal attack on traditional public education in America—an attack that needs to take place until we no longer attempt to fit every child into the same box. And that is the most exciting aspect of charters: they understand that there is more than one way to engage and invigorate a child.

Charters have a much greater tendency to be more holistic and methodical in their approach to each child, and to have nurses, social workers, and counselors on staff. The successful charters have shown themselves to be capable of providing continuity. There's little of the rushed feeling of dealing with a case file, and more of an emphasis on a solid relationship between caregiver and child. In some traditional schools, not only are some key staff such as nurses and counselors overwhelmed with the large number of students, they are even required to split their time among several schools. Because each school is its own entity, charters may have an inherent advantage in dealing with the social services issues. If charter teachers or principals have a problem with a student, rather than simply notifying others to deal with the issue, they can act immediately and proactively to help that child without worrying about the added effort of receiving appropriate signoffs or seeking the authority to speak to certain individuals.

Charter schools may have an advantage in attracting superior teachers because the very nature of the charter school movement affords teachers flexibility and greater autonomy in the classroom. Within the context of a charter school, innovative and creative teachers have the opportunity to express themselves fully. My visits to many of the District's charter schools over the last few years have yielded a far different reality from the one I tend to encounter in traditional public schools. When I visit charters, teachers do not approach me looking for additional resources or supplies. They don't come to me with the same levels of frustration about being shackled in their attempts to do their jobs. In the context of charters, the most common request involves the issue of facilities. What that tells me is that the resource allocation issue that plagues so many traditional school-teachers is not nearly as acute for those who teach in charter schools. Again, that is largely due to the absence of a bureaucracy that siphons resources at the top.

Charters embrace the ideals of private education and the idiom of the marketplace. But charters are not simply an attempt to privatize the public system. They can, in fact, "make public education more democratic by educating all students to be effective citizens without forcing every child into a one-size-fits-all system."[106]

CHAPTER 8

Charters and Challenges

"We cannot learn without pain."

—Aristotle

On the eve of the opening of the 2001–2002 school year, I began to get a number of calls from the press about the D.C. Board of Education's decision to revoke the charters of two public charter schools. As justification for the proposed revocation, the school board cited a number of problems including fiscal mismanagement and impropriety. As I was fielding inquiries from the press about the fairness of the board's actions, I couldn't help thinking about our superintendent Dr. Vance's decision just weeks prior to this to remove the principals from nine under-performing schools that had a history of low test scores and low performance. Dr. Vance had decided to take a "SWAT team" approach and totally revamp the staffs of these schools in an effort to reform them. In reality, some of these schools were so poorly managed that had they not been in the traditional school system they too would have been shut down. It is no secret that traditional public education is fast sinking, and instead of making arrangements for lifeboats, we continue to re-arrange the chairs on the deck. One of the advantages of dealing with problem charter schools is that the charters can always be revoked if they don't live up to their promises.

According to the Center for Education Reform, a relative

handful of charters have failed nationwide. By the end of 1999, thirty-nine schools had closed their doors, representing only 2.3 percent of the nation's more than 1,700 charter schools. In the District of Columbia, since the charter movement began, six school charters have been revoked.[107] Some of these schools closed voluntarily. Others were forced to close because of low student enrollments or administrative or fiscal difficulties. A third category of schools was shut down by their chartering bodies when their charters were revoked due to a variety of reasons including poor management, inadequate educational programs, fiscal or administrative disorder, or misconduct. Far from serving as an indictment of charter schools, these closings only evidence their accountability. Many traditional public schools facing far greater difficulties continue to hobble along to this day.[108]

That charter schools have closed and will close demonstrates the health of the movement and illustrates the most fundamental difference between public charter schools and traditional public schools. These closures demonstrate accountability, one of the charter school movement's greatest strengths and a quality missing in traditional public schools. Barring the ominous mandates of No Child Left Behind with respect to failing schools—which will not go into effect for many years yet (if ever, given large-scale objections from schools nationwide), the worst-performing traditional schools can go on forever, miseducating generation after generation of school children. But in the charter school world, only the strong survive. Those who open a charter school have a contractual obligation to run a good school. If they lack the brains, creativity or drive to do so, they lose their charter.

Charter schools today face different impediments than they did when they first started.[109] While charters continue to grapple with facilities and operational difficulties, political opposition from teachers' unions, state bureaucracies, and local and district offices now pose a much greater menace.

Some of these bodies have been known to insist that charter schools comply with ancient and seldom-enforced regulations, to magnify legislative anomalies, and worse, all in an effort to diminish, delay, or quash charter efforts. And even as charter leaders learn to sidestep these types of sabotage, their opponents' tactics grow more sophisticated and devious.[110]

In one disturbing instance here in the District, facing horrific street traffic that brought out a TV reporter and cameras, the D.C. Public Charter School Board attempted to get information from the traditional public school administration on how to obtain crossing guards. They were told that "crossing guards are not provided for charter schools." Charter schools are public schools attended by children who live in the District of Columbia and they have every right to the protection of crossing guards. Charters continue to struggle to receive those benefits that flow to other public school students. Nationwide, capital financing and a shortage or lack of facilities and start-up and operating funds represent the most significant hurdles for charter schools. Little, if any, capital assistance is available to schools in most instances. In most states, legislators have only just begun to amend laws to grant charters more access to state education funds to help pay for capital and start-up costs such as facilities, purchases, renovations, and construction. In addition, the federal government allocated $175 million in fiscal year 2001 to help with charter schools' start-ups.[111] Some charter schools have shown great creativity in soliciting grants and donations from outside sources, particularly within their local community.[112]

There is another tension in many school districts where charter schools are getting off the ground: The chartering authority entity is usually the local school board, and in many instances charter schools have been rammed down these boards' throats. Most of them tend to be purists who are either hostile to or ambivalent about charter schools. And it is in the shared space and facilities issue where we see the most obstructionist tactics. The rapidly growing charters are at a point where they cannot expand unless they have space. The traditional school bureaucracy is being obstructionist in terms of making space available—even as we continue to press them about it. In the District, excess surplus school properties are still in the hands of the superintendent, the school board, and the mayor. Technically, all "nonsurplus" school properties are within the control of the school board and the superintendent. This includes vacant school properties that may sit unused for years. The school board claims that while it is not using the property, it is holding it for "swing" space. Thus they try to hold onto properties that sit unused, under the theoretical view that they may need them down the road. On the other hand, if the property is listed as a surplus property, it falls under the control of the mayor, who also resists its use by charter schools, arguing that it will be better used for economic development, to achieve a bigger bang for the buck than a school can provide. All the while, charter schools struggle in wretched facilities.

Charter school advocates argue that preference should be given to the educational institutions that are still in existence so that a property can be used in the same way it has been used in the past. I agree with this argument and have in the past introduced legislation that aims to secure both surplus and excess property for educational purposes only. Politically and practically, however, in the District of Columbia and in other jurisdictions around the country, prospective long-term legislative remedies fail to address the immediate short-term needs of charter schools with hundreds of kids on their waiting lists.

By mid-August 2002, there were two excellent charter schools that had yet to resolve their facility issues for the fall, and which would have been unable to open if the issue remained unresolved. These schools are doing good things, but they are caught up in bureaucratic games and cannot find the requisite space. In each instance, the school system promised the school two or three different locations, only to pull the plug at the last minute. But if these schools close, the children return to traditional public schools and so does their money.

These types of issues aside, clearly charter schools are not without flaws, and poor financial oversight is principal among those. Many of the best educators are not good business managers. The charter schools that do work in this respect have the common denominator of a solid team of professionals. That team of professionals provides assistance with financing, facilities, bookkeeping, and any other area where they may be needed. Problems arise when the creative force that assembles the team has some weaknesses, takes a dictator's approach, or ignores advice.

Most jurisdictions that authorize charters have charter school resource boards in place that are generally the links between applicants and authorizing entities. They are the ones who navigate the applicants through the process and provide the initial technical assistance for those interested in starting charter schools. Once the charter is granted, most states' charter school resource boards are not involved in the day-to-day oversight of the individual charter schools' operations. While many states such as New York and California have active charter school associations, ultimately each individual school assumes responsibility for its finances once it receives its charter.

Unfortunately, this is where some charter schools have problems. Since charters are autonomous—operating largely without the bureaucratic oversight of the central administration—they essentially succeed or fail on their own. If an individual charter school does not have the requisite financial checks and balances in place, it is easy for financial mismanagement to occur. A good example is the TechWorld Charter School in D.C. TechWorld was a good idea, whose time many felt had come. The school had a young, enterprising African American visionary who saw the charter school process as a way both to educate high school students and also to catch the wave of the emerging technology industry largesse. The school not only featured computers and computer training for its students, but also had several computer programmers from companies like Microsoft at the school daily, working with students with the goal of having each student fully immersed in the technology revolution. When I first visited the school, I was extremely impressed with the number of private technology partners who were offering their time to assist classroom teachers in their individual classrooms, and the students' openness to the complexities and nuances of the computer world.

Since TechWorld, like other charters, received a significant amount of private financial support in addition to its public dollars, its accounting processes needed to be sound. The founder of the school started to have problems when he began to use school dollars in ways that did not relate directly to the operation of the school. Heady over the school's initial and well-received success, the school's founder began traveling around the country and discussing ways to replicate the TechWorld concept in other cities. In the meantime, the school's hand-picked board of directors essentially allowed him enormous flexibility as it related to managing the school's money. TechWorld had received its charter from the D.C. Board of Education. When the school board began its review of TechWorld's operations, it became clear that significant dollars were not being spent properly. After a detailed investigative process, the school board revoked TechWorld's charter regardless of the fact that from an education standpoint the school seemed well on its way to working. The school board's reason for this revocation was that they had given TechWorld's operating board several opportunities to put the proper financial controls in place, but that the operating board had failed to act.

A valuable lesson to be learned from the TechWorld experience is that charter school autonomy does require accountability on all levels. If a school fails to adhere to all of the promises made in its original charter—particularly in the area of financial management—that school could legitimately close, even if it is educating children.

On a positive note, the TechWorld financial problem came to light as a result of the standardized annual audits that all D.C. charter schools must adhere to. While I strongly believe in the autonomy of the charter schools, we should never lose sight of the fact that they are receiving public dollars. For that reason alone, there must be a regular financial reporting mechanism in place that allows the charter schools' public funders the ability to review individual schools' spending practices.

The idea underlying D.C.'s charter school law, one of the very best in the nation, is that by chartering a significant number of schools each year and closing those that do not perform, after a period of years the District will be home to dozens of very good schools. Unfortunately, over the last three years, D.C.'s chartering boards have become increasingly conservative about chartering schools, fearing that school closure will be misunderstood by the public and reflect poorly on the boards' performance. The liberality of the law's chartering philosophy has been entirely supplanted by an ultraconservative approach based on the principle that no new charter school should be approved unless it can practically guarantee it will not fail. In implementing this philosophy, the boards have greatly expanded the legally mandated application requirements and, instead of welcoming applicants with creative solutions to urban schooling problems, are favoring those who can show that what they want to do has already been done "successfully" elsewhere.

In 2000 and 2001, twenty-eight applications for new public charter schools were submitted to the two boards. There likely would have been many more applications, but in 2000 the Board of Education refused to accept any applications at all. The well-publicized difficulty of finding facilities and the perils of running the chartering gauntlet also suppressed the number of applications.

Of the twenty-eight applicants who decided to press

ahead anyway, only five were approved, an average of 2.5 per year. Yet the D.C. charter school law encourages the creation of up to twenty schools per year. Those who support the public charter schools in the District of Columbia understand the need to prevent unqualified applicants from undermining competent and creative D.C. residents who offer much-needed educational programs.

There will be tensions between the two systems as long as charter schools continue to thrive and students move from traditional schools to charters (and sometimes back). The two sets of schools are, after all, competing for the same pot of tax money.[113] As in any competitive market, there are likely to be some winners and some losers. Ultimately, though, the parents are the ones who will be empowered to do their research and pick the best possible options for their children. Looking for safe havens for their children, parents with limited financial means, who cannot enroll their children in private schools or move to neighborhoods with better schools, have signed on in droves.[114]

CHAPTER 9

Revolution and Education

"Education, then beyond all other devices of human origin, is the great equalizer of the conditions of men, the balance-wheel of the social machinery."

—Horace Mann

This chapter includes a proposal for the fundamental restructuring of child support systems—including schools—starting with children's learning at age three.[115] It includes:

- Clarifying the early care and education picture
- Understanding the beginning school years
- School improvement/education reform through charters
- Using technology to improve education
- Analyzing after-school initiatives
- Moving from school to work
- Preparing for college
- Advancing adult and lifelong learning

No democratic responsibility is more sacred than the care of the young. The nurturing, protection, and education of our youth have been advocated by every serious American thinker, including Thomas Jefferson, Frederick Douglass, Horace Mann, W.E.B. Dubois, John Dewey, Mary McLeod Bethune, John Gardner, James Nabrit, and others. All who fought in the civil rights movement agreed that better education for all American children was the key to a far better American future. When I sought the chairmanship of the Education Committee, I did so because I knew that in our city we had betrayed the best hopes of those who had struggled for that American future.

I worked to find solutions to tragedies we see daily—lost young adults, men without skills and hope, wandering aimlessly and defeated and in what should be the peak of their working years. We see equally unskilled young women minding their toddlers listlessly in the midst of want and decay. We see promising white and Latino and black youngsters growing up in academic isolation, not learning from books but from the lessons and prejudices passed to them in the streets.

I have learned that the current system is not just dysfunctional. Many of its parts excel. Many of its teachers and professionals are deeply committed. But as a system, it is utterly broken. It is not even up to the challenges of the 1970s, '80s, and '90s, much less those presented by the beginning of the twenty-first century.

Ultimately success hinges on the realization of an effective unitary system that also provides choice. At this point, we can start on the path to that success by way of charter schools. Charters offer choice and outputs such as innovation and flexibility that traditional schools have shown themselves unable to provide. What I propose in these pages is not an either-or proposition, but a unified, holistic, and fully integrated vision of an ideal for public education. Fixing what is broken in our schools involves far more than plugging every roof leak and establishing impeccable procurement systems:

- We have not faced the issues of hunger, substandard housing, and abuse and neglect that plague so many of our students.
- We have not faced the challenges presented by a

knowledge-based global economy where people with low-level working skills are becoming economically redundant.

- We have not faced the fact that even total command of the three "R's" is not enough to be competitive in the twenty-first century.
- We are not preparing our students for work in a multicultural, multiracial workplace.

Our profound disappointment in what we have and our fury at the incompetence of the past should make us bold and determined. Sustained efforts by huge numbers of us will solve these problems.

The proposals I put forth here are a first step in a program that will rally parents, citizens, neighborhoods, and communities around a serious revolution in the ways we nurture and educate our children. This is nothing less than a test of our maturity and our competence as citizens. We must rise to this occasion.

I envision a future where our youth, instead of being funneled into traditional high schools and receiving the traditional curriculum, are able to work with teachers, counselors, and parents to identify programs that would best fit their needs and objectives. I anticipate a time when there will be mutual cooperation between administrators of charters and traditional public schools, where there are mutual referrals, joint educational programs, combined parent workshops, sharing of facilities and intercollegiate athletic programs, and ultimately a system where charter schools work in tandem with the traditional school districts.

I also endorse the notion of creating "charters-within-publics"—that is, putting legislation in place that will give the superintendent the power to designate specific charters within the public school system, thereby creating hybrid institutions. These separate mini-charters would operate within the traditional school systems.

In general, the continuum of transformation in our learning systems involves the following:

- Clarifying the Early Care and Education Picture. The care received early in life, including in programs such as universal pre-kindergarten, can profoundly influence later development.
- Understanding the Beginning School Years. A child's first school experiences set the stage for later success or failure.
- School Improvement/Education Reform through Charters. School reform will provide an answer to many of the problems we face in our education system.
- Using Technology to Improve Education. The explosion of technology has broadened the resources available to educators. We need to help develop and implement training programs that prepare prospective teachers to use technology for improved instructional practices and student learning in the classroom. We should try strategies that hold promise for promoting knowledge transfer and use, looking at whether Internet technology and accessibility can improve the process.
- Analyzing After-School Initiatives. Expand after-school programs in some communities and address society's need for greater integration of the learning and social environments. Create partnerships between schools and school districts with other community organizations to create school-based community learning centers that offer educational, recreational, health, and social services to children and adults of all ages.
- Moving from School to Work. Create effective school-to-work systems.
- Preparing for College. Expand national pre-college programs such as Upward Bound that prepare economically disadvantaged students to enter and succeed in college, particularly programs that ready students for academic majors in math and science.
- Advancing Adult and Lifelong Learning. Education makes an important contribution to an individual's ul-

timate well-being. Education and training affect economic success, productivity in the workplace, and the economy as a whole. Develop strategies to advance lifelong learning.

The Core Strategy: Remove Obsolescence and Re-engineer Learning

My proposal calls for the fundamental restructuring of child support systems—including schools—to begin public support for children's learning beginning at age three.

I advocate extending school hours and days to provide the critical educational support our children need in their formative years so that by grade six they will attain world-class levels of educational achievement. We should settle for nothing less. All elementary-aged children ought to be studying and mastering algebra and geometry beginning in the sixth grade.

My view is to approach children's issues across agency lines, identifying and merging the often conflicting strategies but common goals of the school system, the police, the courts, the public health system, employment seminars, and the foster care system. I call this my SmartStart strategy.

I propose that we engage everyone—families, students, teachers, child agencies, employers, churches, and all citizens—in recrafting the educational mission of our public schools and rebuilding our system to produce new, competitive results. We have been in the spotlight for failure. I want us to be in the spotlight for success. The following are the eight core components of my SmartStart strategy that will achieve success if they are applied forcefully and consistently as guiding principles for a decade or longer:

1. Support early learning beginning at age three.
2. Provide more time for learning to take place.
3. Provide a rigorous curriculum at the elementary level.

4. Implement rigorous curriculum in all high schools.
5. Create smaller schools.
6. Manage special education for positive results.
7. Respect, train, and reward our professional teachers.
8. Collaborate across agency lines to reduce truancy, drug abuse, and crime and violence, and to advance employment opportunities.

No credible democracy can fail to address the rebuilding of our education system. No program for economic development can work without globally competitive schools. No promise of hope for our citizens is credible if it does not begin with nurturing our children and paving their path to productive adulthood in the economy of our future.

Provide child learning at a much earlier age.

A core challenge is to support publicly funded early learning for our children starting at age three. This is where we will start. If we can begin on this premise, and work persistently and consistently, every goal we have for our children, our economy, and our culture will fall into place.

The latest scientific research on how the brain works informs us that a child's brain is at its most active stage of growth from birth to age three. For example, a child learns a language by age two. An adult's potential vocabulary is shaped by words learned before age five. The neurological foundations for later learning of math and logic are set before age four. Moreover, the experience of the child in the first two years of life largely determines how the brain develops into adulthood, along with its overall level of emotional stability.

Waiting until age five to begin formal learning is a dinosaur-like practice that should be eliminated. Age five is too late! We must focus on providing a good basic foundation in the early years of life.

To succeed, we will have to start early and drive slowly,

but we will get there safely and on time. All families, particularly those with limited incomes, must have access to early public learning opportunities for their children. This early start will decrease the cost of successfully educating a student, since the recurring costs for failure would be eliminated. We spend millions of dollars on remediation, compensatory education, security, special education, retaining students, summer school, and incarcerating those who enter the juvenile justice system. Funding early learning will cost taxpayers much less than funding the incarceration of so many of these children later.

We provide the resources necessary to supervise every convicted youth offender. Why should it be so difficult to envisage acceptance of similar responsibility for every child's learning environment, especially when we know the negative consequences and costs associated with failing to do so?

Actions:

1. Begin learning opportunities for our children starting at age three.
2. Hire specially qualified early childhood teachers.
3. Add classroom space to accommodate early childhood learning during transition years.

Provide more time to learn: longer school day, longer school year.

The current school day does not match the nine-to-five workforce realities faced by most parents, who now work outside the home for longer and longer hours. Most juvenile crimes are committed between the hours of three and six in the afternoon. The phenomenon of the "latchkey" child is a reality that requires rethinking the time of day that our public education system provides its services. In the information age, learning is not limited to the schoolhouse walls, the time of day, or the yearly season traditionally designated as the "school day" or the "school year." Our children need more time in school. The current school year does not provide our students with enough time to learn what it takes to succeed in this world.

By way of illustration, the school year in the District of Columbia is 180 days long. In Europe and Japan, students spend as many as 220 to 240 days in school per year. When our students are shortchanged by up to 33 percent of the "time to learn" in their school year, they will suffer during their entire lives trying to meet international standards of performance.

Implement a rigorous curriculum at elementary levels.

Public school students could achieve at much higher levels if the curriculum content provided were of a higher level, taught by teachers who know the subject matter and who engage students in active learning. Higher-level content must be taught in the elementary grades. For example, many public school students in the District begin the study of geometry in the tenth grade, after completing a course in algebra in the ninth grade. Geometry is taught in the sixth grade in many American private schools, and in the more successful public schools. It is considered standard for elementary students in Japan and Europe. When the opportunity to engage in higher-level content is denied in the early grades, we place limitations on a student's ability to learn.

Actions:

1. Implement a rigorous elementary curriculum.
2. Begin the study of algebra and geometry and other high level subjects by the sixth grade.
3. Increase attention to the arts as essential higher-order skills.

Implement rigorous curriculum for all high school students.

The mismatch in our public education system is threatening the ability of the next generation of our children to compete effectively in a global economy. That disparity becomes tragic later in high schools where the curriculum taught is far more advanced than the knowledge and skills possessed by students. Most important, there is a mismatch in the level of excellence our children achieve and the level of excellence achieved regularly by students in other industrialized nations. Only 6 percent of America's high school students study calculus. In Germany, that figure is 40 percent and in Japan, 90 percent!

When our students have the opportunity to compete in advanced public and private schools, they do well. It is in our collective self-interest to give every American child such an opportunity.

I propose to provide a high school education for every student that is competitive with the best in education nationwide—in content, quality, and excellence. But every student need not complete four years of college. Today's high-tech job market requires training and excellence, but not always through a full college degree. Our school system must match the career opportunities emerging nationwide. Every high technology center in America was accompanied by a sustained commitment to creating education excellence at the grade school, high school, technical training, and college education levels. North Carolina's Research Triangle, California's Silicon Valley, Massachusetts' Route 128 Corridor, Maryland's 270 Corridor, and Fairfax County's Dulles complex are all the result of serious sustained public investments in quality education.

If we are to participate in the world-class economy growing at our doorstep, we must do what others have done: We must demand, pay for, and manage a sweeping reconstruction of our public school system. It is not a matter of running our current system more efficiently. We cannot take pride in our children becoming dropouts more quickly.

Actions:

1. Implement a solid core curriculum that all students must complete by age sixteen.

2. Redesign the curriculum to meet students' needs, bringing community stakeholders into the design process.
3. Create new specialty magnet science/math schools.
4. Create computer technology schools.

Create smaller schools.

I call for an embargo on disposing of school properties until plans for smaller schools are finalized. Construction cannot lead instruction. The trend toward building larger school buildings has been determined by architects, not educators. Large construction does not provide real economies of scale. Dollars that are saved by constructing large school buildings are almost immediately lost through additional staffing for administration, security, and the academic and social failure that is so often the result of the isolation and impersonal nature of the large school. Appropriate capital funding must be structured and remain consistently directed toward the construction of smaller school buildings. The recent trend toward creating smaller schools within schools is a step in the right direction.

Students are alienated and anonymous in large schools. Students are lost in an impersonal setting where very few adults, if any, know their names.

A sense of ownership or belonging is not fostered in a school of a thousand or more students. Students do not know their own classmates, and teachers do not know them. Appropriately sized schools are much more likely to become key elements of their neighborhoods and communities.

Parents, employers, and other stakeholders can become players in the school's support network, providing tangible contributions and visible models and mentors for students.

Actions:

1. Create and staff smaller schools.
2. Embargo the disposal of any school properties until a

detailed plan to teach children in human-scale environments is in place.

3. Keep classes small to enable greater interaction between students and teachers; in no case would class enrollment exceed limits set forth in D.C. public school regulations.

Manage special education for positive results.

Special education has become a sinkhole for tax money and troubled children. Spending has skyrocketed while the number of students served remains constant. The whole concept of student re-entry from special education back into mainstream learning has been lost in the shuffle. Management of special education for the seriously impaired is a serious challenge for the public school system. Children who have severe learning disabilities should receive appropriate guidance from teachers or counselors. Too many children with advanced levels of difficulty are in expensive and stigmatized care because our system skills for dealing with problem children are poor.

Rebuilding our school system must include rigorous professional training to spot and deal with troubled children, timely contact and referral services with parents, and strong, consistent collaboration with community resources, including the faith community. This effort cannot occur without facing the backlog of thousands of children awaiting professional evaluation. Reliance on regular system staffing for assessments will never resolve this problem.

I strongly support authorizing payment to assessment resources outside the system, using a competitive case rate by any qualified professional. State governments pay for an enormous amount of specialized education service, including separate classrooms, private schools and residential facilities out of the city. Lack of appropriate management, outdated legal mandates and failure to coordinate information and care between all child service agencies has led to exorbitant costs as well as poor outcomes.

Appropriate and effective care for troubled children can only occur by accepting a system-view of public and private services and resources. Child resources must be brought under a coordinated philosophy and strategy.

Actions:

1. Institute fixed-rate assessment payments to private sector assessment professionals for children at risk for learning disabilities.
2. Manage special education dollars to ensure appropriate care and eliminate waste and duplication.
3. Collaborate with public and private stakeholders in child, youth, and family services to produce a seamless and caring service delivery system for troubled children.

Respect, train, and reward professional teachers.

If the job of teaching is to be more than providing custodial care for children, educators must be helped to educate themselves and to create communities of professionals. Incentives must be implemented to encourage accountability, professionalism, and performance.

Performance measurements that simply measure inputs, such as time clocks, demean professionalism and do not ensure better outcomes. Businesses that succeed in "high labor" industries facing global competition must pay well, invest heavily in continuing professional development, and make sure working environments enhance entrepreneurial attitudes and performance.

I propose increasing spending on professional development for teachers. Personnel costs represent hundreds of millions of dollars, which may be a wasted expenditure if we do not continue to invest in the renewal of this human capital. Professional development must be viewed as mandatory—necessary for protecting our investments paid out as teacher salaries.

Actions:

1. Increase investments for professional development for all school staff.
2. Provide ongoing professional development of teachers and facilitate the development of a community of professionals in schools.
3. Demand excellence.
4. Enlist adjunct teachers from community institutions and professions.
5. Rid the system of unqualified teachers.

Collaborate across agency lines to reduce truancy, drug abuse, crime, and violence.

It is a sad reality of our times that school-aged children use illicit drugs and alcohol. This impacts their ability or willingness to learn and the level of crime and violence among juveniles. There is, however, a relationship between a student's school experience and his or her involvement in drugs, alcohol, and crime. Students who are not successful in school are more likely to cut class, be truant, or drop out all together. Students who are not successfully engaged in school are at greater risk for illicit drug use, crime, and violence. Young women who are academically challenged and engaged in schools are less likely to become teenage mothers and/or enter the juvenile justice system.

Over 80 to 90 percent of our incarcerated juveniles did not have a positive school experience, and most dropped out of school. These students are in our schools for most of the day, and we must address their needs during the time that they are with us. It serves no useful purpose to blame parents, blame society, or blame anyone else, while continuing to maintain the obsolete practices now offered in our public schools, and which these young people reject as other consumers reject a product that does not meet their needs.

Public education must join forces and collaborate with all other agencies and community based organizations addressing the problem of illicit drug use by children. Dollars must be put into re-engineering schools so that they become places where young people want to be, where they can learn and become productive citizens.

Re-engineering our schools is essential. But we must go further. We must fit school services into a community. School is the largest piece of life for a growing child, but it cannot be all of life. We must integrate our work with the work of parents, churches, businesses, and community organizations. We must also collaborate proactively with all agencies charged with responsibilities toward children.

Schools must link with the police, parole officers, youth agencies, health agencies, housing agencies, employment agencies, and welfare agencies. This linkage will substantially reduce confusion, reduce costs down the road, and rescue countless young people.

Actions:

1. Coordinate agencies to combat truancy, juvenile illicit drug use, violence, and crime.
2. Involve students in the redesign of a school that meets their needs.
3. Support engaged learning in the schools, dealing forthrightly with the issues and problems that youth are concerned about.

I believe that we can overcome the politics of education and the partisanship that is a barrier to a holistic approach to teaching our children. Education legislation will be rooted in what's best for the kids, rather than political party interest.

CHAPTER 10

Hope for the Future

"Every child must be encouraged to get as much education as he has the ability to take. We want this not for his sake—but for the nation's sake. Nothing matters more to the future of the country: not military preparedness—for armed might is worthless if we lack the brain power to build a world of peace; not our productive economy—for we cannot sustain growth without trained manpower; not our democratic system of government—for freedom is fragile if citizens are ignorant."

—Lyndon B. Johnson

I once visited a middle school not far from the public housing community in my ward for a National Honor Society ceremony. About ten seventh and eighth graders were being inducted into NHS. One girl—a seventh grader—was sitting in the back row on the stage directly behind me in an old yet neatly pressed skirt and white stockings without shoes. She was self-consciously trying to hide the fact that she didn't have shoes. I later asked one of her teachers why she wasn't wearing shoes. I was told that the child only owned one pair of tattered tennis shoes and no dress shoes. She was so proud of her induction into the honor society that she refused to spoil her day by wearing an old pair of tennis shoes with her nice skirt and blouse. She chose, instead, to attend with no shoes at all. Often it doesn't take much support or a tremendous amount of incentive for our children to be steered in the right direction. What has been most troubling with some of our traditional institutions is that they've failed to give many of our kids any support.

In spite of all the problems found in the American public education system, hope does spring eternal for one primary reason: the resiliency of our children. I have run into countless examples of children who come from dysfunctional home settings and who have received limited, if any, nurturing along the way, and they still have an inner drive to excel and succeed. These children demonstrate daily an indomitable spirit that guides them through hardships. Often the determining factor about their eventual ability to succeed or fail is reduced to one or more positive influences in their life.

Our traditional public education system must recognize that the new realities of our society dictate a dynamic, diversified approach to the way children are taught and treated in our schools. One single approach no longer works with all children. Just as diversity of population is one of the greatest strengths of this country, diversity of educational options and experience will help start meaningful change in public education.

I have several recommendations to quicken the pace of meaningful change in both our traditional and alternative public system:

- Recognition and wide-scale diffusion of educational and operational best practices
- The immediate easing of certain bureaucratic requirements on our traditional public schools
- More technical and monetary assistance
- Increased and meaningful links between traditional and alternative public schools to drive reform in both directions

The partisan debates often hold that the charter school experiment is an either/or proposition: Either you favor charters or you prefer traditional public schools. I disagree with this type of zero sum game approach. I am comfortable with the proliferation of charters for a few reasons: Many of them are effective in teaching our children; they are providing families with choice in their children's education; and, perhaps most important, they are in effect forcing the hands of traditional public schools to reform.

The key is in recognizing that we must change our approach to educating our children in this country. Change is difficult—but in this case, it is essential and the right thing to do. As noted educator Howard Fuller says, "As hard as change is, when you are right you must persevere because you will ultimately prevail." In an ideal world and years down the line, perhaps the charters and traditional schools will converge to form a unitary system where they are largely reform-driven and indistinguishable in their characteristics. For the moment, however, charter schools are serving an important purpose. The best of them are allowing for the coordination in one central location of desperately needed services for students, parents, and community members. They are gaining access to children at an early age and identifying their interests. They are providing a system that is malleable enough to respond to children's needs. They are, in short, filling a void left by the traditional public school system.

Until that void is completely filled, local and national policymakers must continue to be open-minded toward charter schools, as well as to reform measures that ensure creativity and innovation. Our children deserve nothing less.

APPENDIX:
WASHINGTON, D.C.
PUBLIC CHARTER SCHOOLS

Chartered by the D.C. Board of Education

Barbara Jordan
Booker T. Washington
Children's Studio School for the Arts
Community Academy
Elsie Whitlow Stokes Community
Hyde Leadership
IDEA—Integrated Design and Electronics
Ideal Academy
JOS-ARZ
KIMA—The Kamit Institute
LAMB—Latin American Montessori Bilingual
The Next Step
Options
Roots
The Village Learning Center

Chartered by the D.C. Public Charter School Board

Arts and Technology Academy
Capital City
Carlos Rosario
Cesar Chavez
D.C. Preparatory Academy

Eagle Academy
The Friendship Edison Schools (four campuses)
Howard Road Academy
KIPDC/KEY Academy
Marriott Hospitality
Maya Angelou
Meridian
New School for Enterprise and Development
Paul Jr. High
SAIL—The School for Arts in Learning
Sasha Bruce
SEED—School for Education Evolution and Development
Southeast Academy
Thurgood Marshall Academy
The Tree of Life
Tri-Community
Washington Math, Science, and Technology
WVSA Auto Arts Academy Public Charter School (recently chartered, to open in 2004)
The District of Columbia Bilingual Public Charter School (recently chartered, to open in 2004)
E.L. Haynes Public Charter School (recently chartered, to open in 2004)
Two Rivers Public Charter School (recently chartered, to open in 2004)

END NOTES

Chapter 1

1. Arianna Huffington, *If It's Broke, Don't Fix It*, www.ariannaon line.com (May 7, 2001).

2. The highest poverty districts received less local general revenues per student than the lowest poverty districts in 1999–2000. While state general revenues and categorical funds tend to compensate for these lower amounts, they do not offset all of the differential in local general funding across districts. *The Condition of Education 2003 in Brief*, National Center for Education Statistics, U.S. Department of Education, Institute of Education Sciences. Also see *The Funding Gap: Low-Income and Minority Students Receive Fewer Dollars*, a fascinating 2002 report by the Education Trust which documented large funding gaps between high and low-poverty and minority districts in many states. The report revealed that in most states, school districts that educate the greatest number of low-income and minority students receive substantially less state and local money per student than districts with the fewest low-income and minority students.

3. Jencks & M. Phillips (Eds) *The Black-Euro-American Test Score Gap* The Brookings Institution Press, Washington, D.C. (1998) cited in Oscar Barbarin, *Ready or not! African American Males in Kindergarten* in *The African-American Male in American Life and Thought*, N.Y. Nova Science Publishers (2001).

4. Jay P. Greene, Ph.D., *High School Graduation Rates in the United States*, Black Alliance for Educational Options & Center for Civic Innovation (November 2001).

5. Mikel Holt, author of "Not Yet 'Free at Last!'" (Institute for Contemporary Studies), as quoted in Jodi Wilgoren, *Young Blacks Turn to School Vouchers as Civil Rights Issue*, (October 9, 2000). See also, A. Huffington, *Just a Test: Bush's Inadequate Education Plan*.

6. In 1999, 16 percent of all children between the ages of 5 and 17 lived below the poverty line. The concentration of poverty among all school-aged children varied by the "urbanicity" of school districts in which they lived; that is, twenty-four percent of children in school districts

in central cities of large metropolitan areas lived in poverty, followed by 20 percent of children living in school districts in central cities within midsize metropolitan areas. *The Condition of Education 2003 in Brief,* National Center for Education Statistics, U.S. Department of Education, Institute of Education Sciences.

7. Arianna Huffington, *Just a Test: Bush's Inadequate Education Plan,* www.ariannaonline.com, (April 16, 2001).

8. From a 1999 survey by the Joint Center for Political and Economic Studies, quoted in Jodi Wilgoren, *Young Blacks Turn to School Vouchers as Civil Rights Issue,* October 9, 2000. See also Huffington, *Just a Test.* Also see Black Alliance for Educational Options, www.baeo.org.

9. Huffington, *Just a Test;* also see Black Alliance for Educational Options, www.baeo.org; also quoted in Salon.com at www.salon.com/politics/feature/2001/04/16/education/.

10. Newark, NY Councilman Cory Booker, quoted in *Just a Test: Bush's Inadequate Education Plan,* Arianna Huffington, (April 16, 2001).

11. Huffington, *Just a Test.*

12. "School Choice is Widespread—Unless You're Poor," from an April 19, *Washington Post* letter to the editor, by Howard Fuller, Superintendent of the Milwaukee Public Schools from 1991–1995; "Letting Parents Decide," *Washington Post* (June 28, 2002); see also Black Alliance for Educational Options at www.schoolchoiceinfo.org.

13. Granted that some young Internet entrepreneurs may not have formal college degrees, but those youngsters, in particular, are highly literate, have proficiency in basic areas, and obviously expert-level skills in technical matters. A good number of these young entrepreneurs hail from affluent families and backgrounds; many of them are literate and technically skilled from a very young age.

Chapter 2

14. See *Hobson v. Hanson,* 269 F. Supp. 401 (D.D.C. 1967), aff'd in part and appeal dismissed in part sub. nom. *Smuck v. Hobson,* 408 F.2d 175 (D.C. Cir 1969).

15. For 100 years, Washington D.C. was run locally by three commissioners who were appointed by the President of the United States. The commissioners were responsible for basic city services and oversaw those who ran D.C. schools. The commissioners perpetuated segregation in the education system, which had its own inherent deficiencies in this tracking approach.

16. In 1995, Congress put the control board in place for two reasons: Because the city had a $500 million deficit and because Marion Barry was

reelected. When Barry was reelected, the Congress did not want him to run the city or have power. The control board was specifically in charge of the city's finances, but it also had the authority to take over schools—which it did.

17. The school board was not disbanded. The board members continued to be elected and hold meetings, but they had little power. Their authority was vested in the trustees appointed by the control board.

18. For an explanation of why the District has two distinct charter school authorizing bodies, see chapter 6.

19. Edison Schools is the country's leading private manager of public schools. It opened its first four schools in August 1995.

20. At the end of 2003, Superintendent Paul Vance resigned and was replaced by Interim Superintendent Elfreda W. Massie. At press time, the mayor and the D.C. Council were in the midst of evaluating the effectiveness of the hybrid school board in place since 2000. Recognizing that mayors in major cities such as Chicago, New York, Boston, and Cleveland have all recommended more mayoral control over local schools, Mayor Williams has recommended that the D.C. school board report to him and be a cabinet-level position. The city council, working through my committee, will resolve this issue in 2004.

Chapter 3

21. That is, longer hours; a longer school year; smaller classes; flexible scheduling; intensive contact with families, if they exist, and extra support for students if they do not.

22. As defined by the District of Columbia during the Patricia Roberts Harris School experiment, the term *community hub* refers to a DCPS building used as a multipurpose center that provides the opportunity to integrate support services and enable intergenerational uses to meet the lifelong learning needs of community residents. The concept includes family and community services, before and after school care, counseling, tutoring, vocational training, art and sports programs, housing assistance, family literacy, health and nutrition programs, parent education, employment assistance, adult education, and access to technology.

23. And indeed, studies have shown that when parents are committed to upgrading their personal education status, there is a natural spillover to their children. A 2000 study of lifelong learning and family literacy showed that children who are involved with their parents in family literacy projects, there has been an increase in the success level of the children in school and a marked decrease in those children's dropout rates.

24. This chapter owes much to Stephanie M. Smith and Jean G. Thomases, *CBO Schools: Profiles in Transformational Education: The Story of 11*

schools where lives and communities are being changed every day. The Academy for Educational Development Center for Youth Development and Policy Research (2001).

Chapter 4

25. The Education Trust. www.edtrust.org.

26. *Committee Report,* District of Columbia Board of Education, Committee on Operations and Vision (November 1, 2002).

27. In particular, Councilmember Sandy Allen, the chair of the Human Services Committee on the D.C. Council, has aggressively pushed city social services agencies to work more closely with D.C. Public Schools.

28. Billionaire financier and philanthropist Ted Forstmann, co-founder of the Children's Scholarship Fund, quoted in Huffington's *Just a Test.*

29. Cited in Bruce Goldberg, *Why Schools Fail,* Cato Institute (1997).

30. See Huffington's *Just a Test: Bush's Inadequate Education Plan.*

31. Since 1997, the city leadership has given teachers several raises that have brought their salaries almost level with teachers throughout the metropolitan region.

32. Congress is one of the obvious practical limitations to labor's clout in the District. Congress can sign off on all of the city's laws and its budget. The Republicans' control of Congress since the early 1990s has helped diminish the influence of labor.

33. Nationally, it has been suggested that teachers' unions in particular often fuel the failures in traditional school bureaucracies. For a scathing indictment of education unions, see Paul Craig Roberts, "Education's Nemesis" (February 18, 2003), reviewing Peter Brimelow, *The Worm in the Apple: How the Teachers Unions Are Destroying American Public Education.* Also see Joe Klein, "How the Unions Killed a Dream: A Philanthropist Withdraws His Offer to Donate $200 Million to Detroit's Inner City Public Schools." *Time Magazine* (October 26, 2003).

34. Encouraging developments include a recent proposal by the New York City teachers' union to do away with the bulk of the work rules that have long enraged city leadership, in exchange for teachers having a greater voice in how their individual schools are run. The proposal would discard traditional union rules relating to length of classes and amount of teacher preparation time, and permit the staff to form school-based management teams, made up of teachers, administrators, and parents, in order to develop policies along with the principal. David M. Herszenhorn, "Teachers Barter with Work Rules," *New York Times* (September 16, 2003).

35. See www.edisonschools.com.

36. David Evans, "Trouble Looms for Edison Schools Founder," *Phil-*

adelphia Inquirer (August 9, 2002); *Data lacking on Edison, for-profit education,* CNN.com (October 31, 2002).

37. Lowell Millken, chairman of the Millken Family Foundation, cited in Huffington, *Just a Test.*

38. See Huffington, *Just a Test.*

39. The New Teacher Project is a revenue-generating nonprofit consulting group that partners with school districts, states, and other educational entities to enhance their capacity to recruit, select, train, and support outstanding new teachers: www.tntp.org.

40. The writers' survey of more than 300 applicants who withdrew from the hiring process revealed that the applicants "had significantly higher undergraduate GPAs, were 40 percent more likely to have a degree in the teaching field, and were significantly more likely to have completed educational work than new hires." Jessica Levin & Meredith Quinn, *Missed Opportunities: How We Keep High-Quality Teachers Out of Urban Classrooms,* The New Teacher Project (2003). See also, Jay Mathews, "Report: Urban Schools Missing Chance to Hire Top Talent," *Washington Post* (September 23, 2003).

41. There have been a number of successful principal recruitment and training efforts in the past several years. One of my personal favorites is New Leaders for New Schools, founded by a dynamic young man named Jon Schnur. New Leaders aggressively recruits talented individuals and trains them to become urban school principals through a rigorous, hands-on training that includes tuition-free coursework, a yearlong full-time residency with a talented mentor principal, and state certification needed to become a school principal. New Leaders places its graduates in urban public schools, including both district and charter schools. See *www .nlns.org.*

42. *National Adult Literacy Survey,* Educational Testing Service (1992).

43. Whether discussing food services or textbook distribution, teachers and principals consistently have given me the best information and advice about our schools' needs. They are always able to offer the right suggestions about how to deal with practical problems—suggestions that have often been ignored by their supervisors or are caught up in the school bureaucracy. Teachers have also approached me most consistently about their students' personal problems—not having resources to participate in a school event, problems with parents or drugs, a child not being adequately clothed or not receiving adequate nutrition.

44. Opponents of the increased push for standardized testing hold that such testing ignores the growing diversity among American students, noting that there is no such thing as a typical American student. They also note that the push forces teachers to teach to the test, rather than engaging in true teaching and learning pursuits in the classroom. Greg Botelho,

Standard operating procedure: Will testing push leave children behind or move them ahead? CNN.com (August 20, 2003).

45. Helyn Trickey. *All-American education: Does it make the grade?* CNN.com

46. See *Back to School: The American Student,* CNN.com Special Report (September 2, 2003); also see testimony of Superintendent Vance before the D.C. City Council.

47. Also see Huffington, *If It's Broke, Don't Fix It.*

48. The National Conference of State Legislatures (NCSL) may be considering the possibility of challenging No Child Left Behind based on the law's ban on imposing unfunded mandates on states. The National Education Association is also considering a lawsuit. See *Education law tries thin state budgets,* CNN.com (July 30, 2003).

49. Perry Bacon, Jr., "Struggle of the Classes," *Time Magazine,* September 22, 2003. See also Sean Loughlin, *Bush cites improvements in America's schools; Democrats say administration falls short on funding,* CNN.com (June 10, 2003); Jerry Parks, "No Illusion Left Behind," *Washington Post* (September 21, 2003).

50. For such things as administrative activities, development and administration of assessments, technical assistance, monitoring programs, data collection and reporting, implementation of school improvement programs, transportation for choice, identifying supplementation services, and increasing parental involvement.

51. Testimony of Dr. Paul L. Vance, Superintendent, District of Columbia Public Schools for the Hearing on No Child Left Behind Act before the Council of the District of Columbia, December 18, 2002.

52. Despite a substantial boost in Title I funding ($34.9 million in FY02, a 31 percent increase), NCLB's accountability provisions will also accelerate budget pressure. Cost drivers include: (a) Choice: The District will have to spend up to the equivalent of 20 percent of Title I, Part A funds for supplemental services and transportation for schools failing AYP for three years; (b) Technical assistance: The D.C. allocation currently yields about $55,000 per school identified for improvement. As more schools are identified, the demand for assistance may outpace the allocation; (c) Tests: D.C. must develop or purchase a new standardized test. In addition to buying or constructing the test, costs will include alignment with standards, field-testing, and training for classroom implementation; (d) Teacher quality: NCLB requires certification and/or proof of subject-area expertise in core subjects. It also requires that paraprofessionals have two-year degrees or pass competency tests. This implies recruiting/training costs, plus new systems for keeping track of credentialing; (e) Data management: NCLB sharply increases the quantity and complexity of data to be managed and reported. The Consolidated Plan describes DCPS's

new web-based Student Academic Database; whatever the initial outlays for this system, there will be a need for ongoing training—not just in system operation, but more importantly, in how to use data to drive program decisions; and (f) Services to special populations: Because all subgroups must make AYP, achievement of limited English proficient and special-education students must increase. More students will take grade-level tests (which may require translators, calculators, or other accommodations), and low-achieving groups will need targeted assistance to improve performance. (The foregoing is thanks to the brilliant, encyclopedically inclined Nelson Smith.)

53. According to the National Conference of State Legislatures (NCSL), school budget crunches have been a national trend for the past few years, with no light at the end of the tunnel. Joseph Van Harken, *Budgets cut student experience,* CNN.com (September 8, 2003).

54. See Jay Mathews, "To Educators, 'No Child' Goals Out of Reach" *Washington Post* (September 16, 2003).

55. Perry Bacon, *Struggle of the Classes.*

56. See Marnie Hunter, *No time to study timely events: Increased interest, little time to discuss world news,* CNN.com (September 8, 2003).

Chapter 5

57. I do believe that charter schools can coexist with traditional schools with thriving unions. Indeed, some jurisdictions like Florida permit teachers who teach in charter schools to decide whether they want to be covered by the district bargaining agreements, negotiate as a separate unit with the governing body, or work independently. Ultimately, I envision teachers themselves being the catalyst for diffusing tensions between the unions and charter schools. As more and more teachers see the value of a less bureaucratized system and as increasing numbers of teachers move back and forth between the traditional school system and charters, there should emerge more of an inclination toward cooperation rather than an increased hostility between the unions and charters.

58. Just about every year, Republicans try to pass a voucher bill. In 1998 the bill passed both the House and Senate, but was vetoed by President Clinton. It was resurrected again each year until it passed in 2003.

59. See also, Spencer S. Hsu, "Feinstein Will Endorse D.C. Vouchers," *Washington Post* (September 4, 2003). For another interesting article, see Spencer S. Hsu, "Two Passionately Involved Parents, One Divisive Issue," *Washington Post* (September 14, 2003).

60. Unlike charters, which are actually public, private schools are not accountable for performance to any public body. They may also be selective about their enrollment.

61. For a rebuttal to these allegations, see Howard Fuller & Kaleen Caire, *Lies and Distortions: The Campaign Against School Vouchers,* Marquette University's Institute for Transformation of Learning (April 2001).

62. I agree with Mayor Williams, who was quoted as saying: "I know this is a controversial issue. We're not saying this is something the entire country ought to do. But we are saying for the next five years, this is a useful initiative and experiment here in this city to complement the reforms that are already underway." "Feinstein Will Endorse D.C. Vouchers," *Washington Post* (September 4, 2003).

63. Although often overlooked, home schooling as an option has steadily progressed to become one of the fastest growing forms of school choice. Estimates of children taught at home range from 850,000 to 2,000,000, depending on the source. *More families opting for home schooling,* CNN.com (September 3, 2003).

64. This consensus was developed at the 1990 World Conference on Education for All in Jomtien, Thailand. See Lavinia Gasperini, *The Cuban Education System: Lessons and Dilemmas,* The World Bank, LCSHD Series (vol.48, December, 1999). This chapter also benefits from: Dr. Abida Ripley, *Charter Schools and Their Impact on Reading and Writing.*

65. See Joe Nathan, *Charter Schools: Creating Hope and Opportunity for American Education* (1996) for one of the pre-eminent works on charters.

66. Charter School Law: Comparative Perspectives of the Role of the Sponsor. Fellowship Colloquium, Program on Law and State Government, Indiana University School of Law–Indianapolis (June 23, 2003).

67. Jodie Morse-Mesa, *Do charter schools pass the test?* CNN.com (May 28, 2001); *The National Charter School Directory 2003,* Center for Education Reform (2003).

68. Marc Fisher, "To each its own: Are charter schools providing customized education, a breakdown in curricular coherence or both? A tour of five charters in the District provides a glimpse of the implications," *Washington Post* (April 8, 2001).

69. See Fisher, "To Each Its Own."

70. For more information about each state's charter school laws, see the Center for Education Reform website at www.edreform.org.

71. Charles Abelman, *Charter Schools in the District, Notes from the D.C. Public Schools,* World Bank (December 1, 1998).

72. See, for example, Nancy Trejos, "Latino Leaders Want Pr. George's Charter: Group Seeks New Hyattsville School to Assist Growing Hispanic Population." *Washington Post* (September 17, 2003).

73. Research has shown that small schools permit closer connections between teachers and students and foster greater achievement, safety, and satisfaction than large public high schools. These smaller schools also record higher graduation rates than the national average for students at-

tending public high schools. In late 2003, the Bill and Melinda Gates Foundation donated almost $52 million to create sixty-seven new small schools in New York City. See Laura Fording, "Thinking Small: Many large urban public high schools are failing their students. Is downsizing the answer? *Newsweek* (September 22, 2003).

74. See Fisher, "To Each Its Own."

75. Stephanie M. Smith & Jean G. Thomases, *CBO Schools: Profiles in Transformational Education*, AED Center for Youth Development & Policy Research.

76. See Charles Abelman, *Charter Schools in the District, Notes from the D.C. Public Schools*, World Bank (December 1, 1998).

77. Dr. Vance noted in the same article that charter schools are really not the problem and that if traditional public schools were doing their jobs, then they would have nothing to be concerned about in terms of charter schools taking kids away from them. If public schools were effective, then fewer parents and children would find charter schools an attractive alternative. Since public schools are not doing their jobs, charter schools are increasingly successful. Dr. Vance even offered the enlightened position that perhaps the public school system can learn from the charters and mirror some of their offerings. "What I've heard about the charters is that they don't have to deal with insensitive bureaucracy. They have supplies and materials. They teach with few, if any, interruptions. They teach where no one loses sight of the main thing, which is teaching and learning. They aren't bogged down with conflicting directives from central administration. The teachers who have gone from our schools to charters have found the freedom and collegiality, which they were promised. There's a siphoning off of our talented and competent teachers and administrators. They saw an opportunity to do what they had dreamed of doing, to become unshackled." Fisher, "To Each Its Own." *Washington Post* (April 8, 2001).

78. Fisher, "To Each Its Own."

79. Center for Education Reform, *Charter Schools Today: Changing the Face of American Education* (February 8, 2000).

80. Data courtesy of Center for Education Reform at www.edreform .org; responses were received from 305 of the 1,208 charters operating as of June 1999 in twenty-three states and the District of Columbia. According to CER, theirs was the largest sample to date of activity in and around charter schools nationwide. Center for Education Reform, *Charter Schools Today: Changing the Face of American Education* (February 8, 2000).

81. Councilmember Lightfoot was instrumental in promoting the charter schools when he was on the council. He became one of three people who pushed forward the charter school legislation.

82. *Children in Crisis: A Report on the Failure of D.C.'s Public Schools*, Na-

tional Association of Educational Progress (1996); see also Fisher, "To Each Its Own."

83. Currently both bodies operate in the District: fifteen charters have been granted by the D.C. school board; twenty-five by the public charter school board. To their credits, both bodies have gone to great lengths to ensure accountability, and the application processes have been equally rigorous. In the District, it is possible for up to twenty new charter schools to open each year.

84. Not long after retiring from D.C. Public Schools, Linda McKay joined the Public Charter School Board and was responsible for, among other things, reviewing applications for charter schools.

85. Justin Blum, "Graduating with Distinction: From a Shaky Start, D.C. Charter School, Students Achieve Success," *Washington Post* (May 31, 2002).

86. News Release (August 30, 2001).

87. PCSB supervised a total of sixteen schools on nineteen campuses in that year. The Carlos Rosario School was excluded from these results because it is an adult program. In addition, five other schools were in their first year and thus were excluded from the rankings.

88. In evaluating Stanford-9 results, the board used a variety of analytical strategies including proficiency levels, percentiles, NCE scores, gain scores, and percentile gains.

89. The foregoing charter school gains are from *School Performance Reports, District of Columbia Public Charter School Board, November 2002 for Academic Year 2001–2002.*

Chapter 7

90. In *CBO Schools: Profiles in Transformational Education*, the Academy for Educational Development highlights the following principles and practices as being shared by effective and outstanding community schools: (1) High and comprehensive standards; (2) relevant and diverse learning opportunities; (3) personalized and flexible learning environments; (4) supports and services for effective learning; and (5) opportunities to make a contribution.

91. Sadly, Americorps, long favored by Bush, has suffered devastating cutbacks, which have drastically reduced its number of volunteers. See Jeffrey Selingo, "Americorps cuts back on volunteers, promoting concern for local programs," *Chronicle of Higher Education* (May 27, 2003).

92. The average D.C. charter school enrolls less than 260 students.

93. This section adapted from testimony before the Committee on Education, Libraries, and Recreation (October 19, 2002).

94. The SEED Foundation. *The SEED Public Charter School 1998–2000 Annual Report.*

95. *Cesar Chavez Public Charter High School for Public Policy Annual Report 2000–2001.*

96. Cesar Chavez mission statement.

97. Chavez's remarkable list of partners also includes: College Bound to provide college-prep mentoring, Choice USA, D.C. Agenda, Georgetown University's Public Interest Center, Leadership Conference on Civil Rights–Immigrant Policy, Senate Democratic Policy Committee, Sierra Club, SIECUS, Student Conservation Association, United Students against Sweatshop Labor, US Public Interest Research Group, Washington Peace Center and the White House Office of the Vice President–Office of Domestic Policy, Council for Latino Agencies, National Parks Conservation Association, Alliance for Justice, Sierra Club Environmental Justice, Educational Trust, Choice USA, Youth Venture, Department of Energy, Department of Housing and Urban Development, Food and Drug Administration, Department of Transportation, Ophelia's House, Sarah House, Latin America Youth Center, Calvary Multicultural Child Development Center, Upper Cardoza Health Services, Edward Mazique Child and Family Center, and Joy of Sports Foundation.

98. Gail Russell Chaddock, "Three teachers and lots of hope: Ambitious charter school aims to instill a love of learning and reinvent urban schooling." *The Christian Science Monitor* (December 22, 1998).

99. See also Justin Blum, "Graduating with Distinction"; Marc Fisher, "Chavez Seniors Find Hard Work Very Rewarding." *Washington Post* (June 4, 2002).

100. See *Carlos Rosario International Public Charter School Annual Report, School Year 2000–2001.*

101. The Rosario Center was the winner of an excellence award given by the U.S. Department of Education in 1993, having exceeded all major expectations on a nationwide basis.

102. *Can Charter Schools Save the Kids? A Study of At Risk Youth Education in Washington, D.C.*

103. Adopted from testimony before the D.C. Council Committee on Education, Libraries and Recreation (October 19, 2002).

104. The school does not have weekend boarding capacity.

105. Fisher, "To Each Its Own."

106. Bates College professor Stacy Smith, cited in Fisher, "To Each Its Own."

Chapter 8

107. The charter of the Marcus Garvey Public Charter School was revoked by the D.C. Board of Education in 1998 because of the leader-

ship's non-adherence to generally accepted accounting principles, fiscal mismanagement, and other violations of charter conditions. Young Technocrats and New Vistas were revoked in 1999 and 2001, respectively, for engaging in a pattern of non-adherence to generally accepted accounting principles. TechWorld Public Charter School's charter was revoked by the Board of Education in 2002 for failure to adequately maintain basic accounting records and inadequate cash management controls, among other things. Also revoked in 2002 were World Public Charter School and Richard Milburn Charter School, both for committing a material violation of the conditions, terms, or standards of charter conditions.

108. Center for Education Reform, *Charter Schools Today: Changing the Face of American Education* (February 8, 2000).

109. A recent CER survey of charter schools found that 38 percent regarded funding to be their biggest challenge and 21 percent regarded facilities as their biggest concern. A recent report by Policy Analysis of California Education held that some charters are also facing many of the same problems plaguing traditional public schools, such as insufficient funding and a lack of resources for serving needy students, and warned that unless "charter enthusiasts can escape deep-seated structural constraints, these independent schools may reproduce stratified layers of student performance, just like garden-variety public schools." Hattie Brown, "Charter Schools Found Lacking Resources," *Education Week* (April 16, 2003).

110. Center for Education Reform, *Charter Schools Today: Changing the Face of American Education* (February 8, 2000).

111. The average state receives between $2 and $3 million, with some states receiving as much as $10 million or more per year.

112. Center for Education Reform, *Charter Schools Today: Changing the Face of American Education* (February 8, 2000).

113. Fisher, "To Each Its Own."

114. Jodie Morse-Mesa, *Do charter schools pass the test?* CNN.com (May 28, 2001).

115. This chapter was developed in collaboration with Dawn Arno and Johnny Allem.

REFERENCES

Blum, Justin. Teachers Union Official on Leave; Scandal Tainted Interim President. *Washington Post* (March 20, 2003).

Carter, Samuel Casey. *No Excuses: Lessons from 21 High-Performing, High-Poverty Schools.* Heritage Foundation.

"If I Can't Learn From You . . ." Ensuring a Highly Qualified Teacher for Every Classroom. Quality Counts 2003, *Education Week* (January 9, 2003).

Lengel, Allan, & Valerie Strauss. Teachers Fret Over Pace of Union Probe; 'Closure' Critical to Stabilizing, Reforming Organization, Members Say. *Washington Post* (June 25, 2003).

Stern, Sol. *Breaking Free: Public School Lessons and the Imperative of School Choice,* Encounter Books (2003).

Tucker, Neely. Another Guilty Plea in D.C. Union Probe. *Washington Post* (April 12, 2003).

Tucker, Neely. Ex-Driver Pleads Guilty in Probe of D.C. Union; Defendant Admits Cashing Checks Worth $1.2 Million. *Washington Post* (February 7, 2003).

Tucker, Neely. Teachers' Union Oversight Criticized. *Washington Post* (May 1, 2003).

Tucker, Neely, & Justin Blum. Ex-District Official with Ties to Union Charged in Scandal. *Washington Post* (April 3, 2003).

ACKNOWLEDGMENTS

I have been fortunate and blessed throughout my life. This book represents another example of those blessings. A world of thanks to Amanda Enayati, who helped to bring my words to life and made all of this a reality. In addition, I recognize that none of my success would have been possible without the love and support of my family and friends. I especially thank my wife, Beverly Bass Chavous, who continues to support me and my public service. I thank my sons, Kevin and Eric, of whom I am proud beyond words. I sometimes feel as though I was put on this earth just to make sure that they were born. Thanks to my parents, Harold and Bettie Chavous; my sisters, Estella and Rose Chavous; my brother, Edwin Chavous; my sister- and brother-in-law Barbara and Lou Loretz; sister-in-law Tracey Chavous; and brother-in-law, Michael McCorkle. Thanks to Friason and Betty Travis; Fran and Emma Burwell, Bill Maultsby, and Donnie James. Thank you to a host of extended family members who have always supported me.

Thanks to lifelong friends Dr. John Armstead, Maurice Boler, Lisa Morrison Butler, Bob Knowling, Joseph Mims, Steve Williams and my best friend, Bryan Williams.

Thank you, Indianapolis Public School #43, St. Thomas Aquinas Elementary, Brebeuf Preparatory High School, Wabash College and the Howard University School of Law for giving me a quality education.

Thank you Bill Robinson.

My law firm, Sonnenschein Nath & Rosenthal LLP has been extraordinarily supportive. Thanks to my law firm colleagues Amy Bess, Brett Hart, Singleton McAllister, Elliott Portnoy, Cap Potter, Duane Quaini, Christopher Smith, Reed Stephens, and Errol Stone.

Thank you to those who served as professional mentors and helped shape my professional career: the late John Breit, the late Robert Cadeaux, Frank Carter, Conrad Fontaine, the late Byron K. Hollett, Joe Jaudon, Ronald Jessamy, Harold Jordan, W. Gary Kohlman, John Mosby, Charles Ogletree, John Sturc, James Taglieri, and Judge Ricardo Urbina.

Thanks to those who helped me understand that public service was more than just politics: Dr. Marie Aldridge, the late Herbert Barksdale, Bertie Bowman, Herb Boyd, Thedas Boyd, Gladys Bray, James Butcher, Sylvia Butler, Lillian Chatman, Milton Chavis, Doug Coe, Erman Clay, Savannah Crook, Ruth Cooper, Father Dalton Downs, Beverly Goode, George Gurley, Richard Hamilton, Willie Hardy, Calvin Hawkins, Reverend Edward Harris, John Hicks, the late James Jefferson, Donna Johnson, Sandra Ford Johnson, Betty Lewis, Virgil McDonald, Barbara McKoy, Sam Morrison, Rose Neverdon, Alberta Paul, Denise Reed, Houston Roberson, Naomi Robinson, Tony Robinson, Ed Rogers, James Short, Linda Jo Smith, Vincent Spaulding, Chester Speight, Rodney Streeter, Bernardyne Williams, and Constance Woody.

Thanks to my political mentors and friends whose counsel I will always value: Johnny Allem, Isaac Fulwood, Jim Hudson, Ron Lester, the late Mayor Walter Washington, Wellington Webb, and former Council colleagues John Ray and Bill Lightfoot.

Special thanks to my colleagues on the Council of the District of Columbia, by far the hardest working local legislature in the country: Chairperson Linda Cropp, Sandy Allen, Sharon Ambrose, Harold Brazil, David Catania, Jack Evans, Adrian Fenty, Jim Graham, Phil Mendelson, Vincent Orange, Kathy Patterson, and Carol Schwartz. I especially want to recognize my Education, Libraries and Recreation Committee members, who, along with Chairperson Cropp and Councilmember Patterson, have devoted themselves to being hands-on in the oversight of our school reform efforts: Councilmembers Ambrose, Schwartz, Mendelson, and Fenty.

Thank you D.C. Mayor Anthony Williams.

Many humble thanks to the people of Ward 7, District of Columbia, who have given me the honor of representing them on the Council of the District of Columbia since 1993.

Thanks to my entire Council staff over the years, who consistently gave of themselves on behalf of the citizens of Ward 7.

Thank you Ward 7 Education Council for all you do for our schools.

Thank you Stedman Graham, Quincy Jones, and Armstrong Williams.

Thanks to Pedro Alfonso, Jim Blew, John Bryant, Kaleem Caire, John Clyburn, H.R. Crawford, Bernard Demczuk, Bud Dogget, Raul Fernandez, Virginia Walden Ford, Terry Golden, Sylvan Gershowitz, C. Boyden Gray, Walter Hamlin, Cathy Hughes, Charlene Drew Jarvis, Jim Kimsey, Reta Lewis, Rusty Lindner, Pepe Lujuan, Jackie Pinckney, James Powell, Joe Robert, Michele Roberts, Jim Shelton, Jeff Thompson, Richard Thompson, and Horace Turner.

A very special thanks to George Lowe and Jack Lyon.

Special recognition to those who helped shape my message and contribute to my views on education policy: my former chief of staff Kathy Etemad, my former Committee Clerks Jerry Johnson and Janene Jackson, Jeanne Allen, Kay Brisbane, Connie Clark, Dr. Howard Fuller, Laura Gardner, Judy Gee, Connie Newman, Thomas Stewart, and Carrie Thornhill.

Thanks to Meredith Attwell, Larry Irving, Leslie Thornton,Cristina Valencia, Sharla Woods, and especially Maurita Coley who urged me to write "what I feel."

This book would not have been possible but for the generosity and assistance of many individuals. Thank you to: Charles Abelman, Eric Adler, Kent Amos, Charlise Baird, Don Brown, Peggy Cooper Cafritz, Robert Cane, Joanne Capper, Jay Castano, Tony Colon, Jacqueline Davis, Cynthia

Diamond, David Domenici, State Senator Dwight Evans, State Senator Eric Fingerhut, James Forman, Sonia Guiterriez, David Harris, Donald Hense, Phyllis Jones, Jack Kemp, Gwen Kimbrough, Senator Mary Landrieu, Brandon Lloyd, State Senator Theresa Lubbers, Cathy Lund, Linda McKay, Shirley Monastra, Education Secretary Rod Paige, Malcolm Peabody, Mayor Bart Peterson, State Rep. Greg Porter, Professor Jamin Raskin, Nina Rees, Irasema Salcido, Jon Schnur, Jane Smith, Nelson Smith, Connie Spinner, Paul Vance, Anna Varghese, Raj Vinnakota, and Raquel Whiting.

Thank you Dawn Arno, the co-architect of SmartStart (Chapter 9) and a superior educator in her own right.

Thank goodness for the steady guidance and counsel of my agent, Lee Doman and the folks at Goldfarb & Associates.

Thank you Noemi Taylor and your colleagues at Capital Books for your confidence in this project.

Finally, sincere thanks and appreciation to all the teachers, principals, and countless caregivers who have dedicated their lives and very beings to serving our children.

Kevin P. Chavous
November, 2003

INDEX